DATE DUE

NOV 2 6 2005	
JAN 6 - 2007	
Feb. 2, 2007	
May 2007	
JAN	
MAR	
MAY 2 7 2008	

D1261286

ZEN AND ZEN CLASSICS
Volume Five

Gathering Firewood, by Sosan

The inscription, by the artist, says:

今日西山大有人，祖師之骨刈成薪，
不知擔上重多少，添得千秋春色新，

Today the Western Mountain is crowded;
They are cutting up the bones of the patriarchs and masters for fuel.
I have no idea what weight [value] their
  burdens may have,
But anyway the great thing is that the
  eternal spring is [once more] new.

The picture shows a large number of Zen
monks carrying brushwood, and seems to be
a satire on the popularity of Zen.
  I could find nothing about Sosan himself.

Gathering Firewood, by Sosan

The inscription, by the artist, says:

今日西山大有人，盡將祖佛以爲薪。
不知擔上重量少，添得青春一番新。

Today the Western Mountain is crowded:
They are cutting up the bones of the patriarchs and masters for fuel.
I have no idea what weight [value] their
burdens may have.
But anyway the great thing is that the
eternal spring is [once more] new.

The picture shows a large number of Zen
monks carrying brushwood, and seems to be
a satire on the popularity of Zen.
I could find nothing about Sosan himself.

R. H. BLYTH

ZEN

AND

ZEN CLASSICS

Volume Five

Twenty-five Zen Essays

THE HOKUSEIDO PRESS

First published, as Volume Seven of
ZEN AND ZEN CLASSICS, 1962
Reprinted as Volume Five 1966

Published by The Hokuseido Press
3-12, Kanda-Nishikicho, Chiyoda-ku, Tokyo

DEDICATED

TO

SUZUKI DAISETZ,

THE ONLY MAN WHO CAN WRITE
ABOUT ZEN
WITHOUT MAKING ME LOATHE IT

PREFACE

There is nothing harder to write about than Zen. No, this is not so. There is nothing harder than really to write, because really to write means to write by Zen. To write, or eat, or sing, or die by Zen is difficult. Really to write about Zen means writing by Zen about writing or eating or singing or dying by Zen. So to write about Zen is not difficult; what is difficult is to write by Zen. And if we don't write by Zen we shouldn't write at all. If we don't live by Zen, there's no point in living.

What is Zen? Zen means doing anything perfectly, making mistakes perfectly, being defeated perfectly, hesitating perfectly, having stomach-ache perfectly, doing anything, perfectly or imperfectly, PERFECTLY. What is the meaning of this PERFECTLY? How does it differ from perfectly? PERFECTLY is in the will; perfectly is in the activity. Perfectly means that the activity is harmonious in all its parts, and fully achieves its proposed end. PERFECTLY means that at each moment of the activity there is no egoism in it, or rather, that our ego works together with the attraction and repulsion of the Egoism of the nature within and without us. Our pain is not only our own pain; it is the pain of the universe. The "joy" of the universe is also our joy. Our failure or misjudgement is that of nature, which never hopes or despairs, but keeps on trying to the end, like Bruce's spider, which failed to fall at last, or like Alfred's cakes, which succeeded in being burnt to a cinder.

Zen is at once irresistibly attractive and unutterably repulsive. Zen draws us to it for many reasons. First, because at last we have a belief which we need not believe in. No dogmas, no ritual, no mythology, no

7

church, no priest, no holy book,—what a relief!

> The sticks break, the stones crumble,
> The eternal altars tilt and tumble,
> Sanctions and tales dislimn like mist
> About the amazed evangelist.
> He stands unshook from age to youth
> Upon one pin-point of the truth.

Second, Zen, even the word itself, enables us to perceive that all our deepest experiences of life, of music, of art, music, poetry, humour and so on, however varied they may be, and deriving as they do from the most widely different circumstances, have all a similar "taste" or odour, a common element that seems fundamental. This idea is of course dangerous in its monistic, scientific, philosophical, unpoetical tendency, and we need all the more to insist upon the variety, the plurality, the disparateness of Zen. But we must have a unity as well as a diversity, and so the word Zen usually refers to this depth of oneness in our depth of life. But just as deep is our experience of difference. For a thing to exist at all it must have this separateness; at the same time it has no existence if only separate. Spengler describes the different "Zens" of the various world cultures, of which, with an instinct of genius (or it may be mere nationalism and misanthropy) he denies the inter-comprehensibility, that is, their essential identity. The same mistake is often made in regard to ego-lessness, in Japanese *mu-ga*. Egolessness alone won't do, and to bring in the Over-Soul or something of that sort won't do either, for if we pinch the Over-Soul it won't shriek. What we want is something unpinchable and pinchable, and the ego is pinchable. So we must have *muga,* and at the same time *yuga,* egofulness; then we are all right, as Shakespeare was when he was Hamlet and at the same time Shakespeare, a Danish prince and an English playwright.

Third (the third reason why Zen is so acceptable), Zen makes us realise that, as Hazlitt said, only "what interests is interesting." Zen is interest. Zen makes the mountains more mountainous, and the valleys more valeful, and yet at the same time the lower the mountain the better, and the shallower the valley. We begin to have an idea of what we have always been looking for without knowing it. When we read a novel or look at a statue or listen to a piano or a piccolo, even if we are ignorant of human nature or form-blind or tone-deaf, we know at least whether it is alive or not, whether it feeds us. Zen is the universal standard of judgement we have all been looking for. Zen is good taste.

What is odious about Zen is what people say about it (all of them with the exception of Suzuki Daisetz); the photographs of Zen monks in their fanaticism, bigotry, superstition, and standardisation; the pettifogging and infantile personal stories supposed to exemplify moments of enlightenment; the commentaries on the *Hekiganroku* and *Mumonkan* or koans, with their esotericism and superiority-complex; foreigners (no exceptions) who pretend to understand Zen, and bamboozle themselves and (some of) their readers by adding their own legs to the snake. Nobody understands Zen; nobody can explain it; writing books about it is effrontery and impertinence. In fact, Zen is itself a kind of impudence. On the other hand it is the essence of modesty, the modesty of nature. Let us combine the two.

When I say what Zen is, or what it isn't, or when I don't say what it is or isn't, it doesn't matter. All that you, the reader, have to do is to agree with it. If I say, "Zen is a mouse when it spins," or, "Zen is a spin when it mouses," what is important is to agree with it whole-heartedly, with pleasure and gratitude, without reservation. Just agree with it, that is all. Or rather, agree with me. Love the good man, not his goodness; hate the bad man, not his badness. Zen means agreeing with everybody and everything, or rather, every thing. When we really "understand" a thing or a person, we agree with it. When we "understand" (the reason for) Communism or Christianity or Capitalism or Calligraphy, or Cabbages or Kings, we agree with it, we will it. Zen means willing all that is. We become like the *higurashi,* the day-darkener, the insect that sings the sun below the distant hills. If it does not cry night will not come. When we will a thing we become it, because a thing is itself by virtue of its "willing" to be what it is, or rather, as the *higurashi* shows us, what it is becoming. When someone agrees with me I know I am wrong. Rightness is unique, incommunicable, inimitable, unshareable, unrepeatable, right for that person in that place at that time only. We must agree with Hitler and with bedbugs, and at the same time disagree with them, and Zen is this at-the-same-time-ness. Thus on the one hand, "Thy will, not mine, be done," and on the other, "My will, not Thine, be done." Everything must be as it is, but everything must be changed from what it is.

Without love, without joy, without humour it is impossible to please God, that is, write about Zen. But the reader also must do his part. Love must receive love, joy must receive joy, humour must receive humour. There is the Zen of giving and the Zen of receiving. It is said that it is more blessed to give than to receive, but blessedness is in any case not a matter of more or less, bless you!

A few of the articles in the present volume have already appeared in *The Young East* and in *Orient / West* (*Today's Japan*). I wish to thank the publishers of these magazines for their kind permission to reprint them. (Actually I didn't ask them.) They have been carelessly revised, and a few mistakes and misprints added.

R. H. Blyth

25 August 1961

CONTENTS

List of Illustrations

ZEN, CHRISTIANITY, AND
BUDDHISM

In some ways there is more Zen about Christianity than Buddhism; certainly there is more Zen to be found in English literature than in Japanese or Chinese literature, and in Indian literature Zen is painfully absent. But first let us consider the fundamental identity of Christianity and Buddhism and Zen, and then take some equally fundamental differences. The essence of Christianity is, Christ died for you. Buddhism teaches that we have the Buddha nature. When you are the universe, there is Zen. But "You have the Buddha nature" means that you are divine, you are one with Christ. "You are the universe" is another way of saying "You are God." Thus Zen may be called the ultimate simplification of both Christianity and Buddhism, the former being clabbered up with emotionalism and theology, the latter entangled in morality and a more or less scientific philosophy.

However, the theology of Christianity is highly symbolical, and since human beings live by metaphors and similes (taken from Nature, "The Great Stereotype"), the dogmas of Christianity may be, should be, and perhaps are (subconsciously) understood in the Zen way. The creation of the universe by God means God's giving up his all-ness, becoming imperfect in order to look at his own perfection, in order to think of himself. It is the Fall of God, of which the creation and fall of Adam is a kind of close-up. The intellect is separated from the rest of the personality and judges it, and thus Christ adjures us, "Judge not!" The state of man (= the universe, God) suffers the nature of an insurrection. The Crucifixion is the giving up of the intellect, the abnegation of reason, "Not my

13

will" meaning, not my idea, not my judgment, not my thought, not thought. But with the Resurrection the intellect is received back from the dead; it rejoins the personality, and never again acts separately from it.

Christianity was lucky in that the Jewish myths and amalgamated cults could be interpreted with the Greek-Alexandrian mysticism—or rather, shall we say that the Early Church and later poets were able to bring out the deeper meaning latent in the Jewish Hymn of Creation and the Eastern mystery religions and agricultural rites. In the case of Buddhism, it took over the prosaic and childish theory of reincarnation, which gave man an immortality with all its disadvantages (lack of responsibility, no recollection of past lives) and none of its advantages (recompense for the useless suffering and injustice of this world, and fulfillment of man's desire not to suffer annihilation). In addition, the hyperboles and excessive ornamentation of the accounts of the Buddhas and Bodhisattvas and their realms of bliss are repulsive to the non-Indian mind, far more so than the anthropomorphism of the Bible.

The difference between Christianity and Buddhism is to some extent a difference of the national character of the peoples who created or embraced those religions. In India, people were overwhelmed by Nature, and sought to escape from the excess of life into a sublime, other-worldly, passionless, almost lifeless condition. All the things of this earth were to them *mayoi* (illusion), in themselves empty, and the cause of fruitless desire in man, desire which is the root of all evil. In Judea, where Nature is not so kind, man was correspondingly grateful for the little he received, and attributed to God his own feelings, "And he saw it was good." Judaism is yea-saying, Buddhism nay-saying. In the life of Christ, as in early Christianity, we feel little of the asceticism that comes, as in the case of Buddha, from a surfeit of good things. In this respect Zen is far closer to Christianity, at least the Christianity of Browning, though Zen would say rather,

"God's in his world, all's right with Heaven."

To Buddha, the world is full of pain, pain that must be escaped from into Nirvana. This Nirvana is an ego-less state in which the illusory individual soul is swallowed up in the (perhaps equally illusory) World-Soul. If "life is suffering," life-lessness can hardly be considered a great evil. Buddha seems never to have thought of the Nirvana of poetry, of art, of music, of nature, of love. For this "illusory" Nirvana of love and hope and glory, the "illusory" soul is necessary, the soul in its painful peace, its peaceful pain. Without pain there is indeed no real painlessness. This is the "peace that passeth understanding," the peace of the Cross. "Take it, for it is all God offers." Here is the one paradox which Zen has always overlooked or avoided. This is perhaps the result of Zazen, which tranquillizes by immobility. We see the same falsity in Buddhist statues, which never eat, never kill mosquitoes even, never have diarrhea, never defend the helpless.

Christ was well aware of pain, but for him more important was evil, religious rather than moral evil, since it consists of alienation from God, which is lack of love. Evil is loneliness. Zen means never being lonely. Loneliness comes when we separate what are really not separated, ourselves and things.

Is God a person? Are you a person? What is a person? Has the universe a mind? According to Wordsworth,

> The Moon doth with delight
> Look round her when the heavens are bare...

Has the universe no mind? Darwin wrote:

> I remember well the time when the thought of the eye made me cold all over.... The sight of a feather in a peacock's tail, whenever I gaze at it, makes me sick.

To explain the universe in terms of material things and mechanical forces only, without any Mind whatever, is indeed as impossible and superstitious as a belief in a kind of Father Christmas deity. On the other hand, animism sees everything as a soul. But this, however poetically true it may be, obscures the distinction between animate and inanimate. No doubt a stone is a person too, but it does not have or wish to have the immortality that human beings desire. The difference between a stone and a man is that a man (a poet, that is, who is the only really human being) knows what a stone is; a stone does not. To know a stone we must do two things. We must know that it is the whole universe; the whole universe is contained in it, and nothing is excluded. It is the Way, the Truth, and the Life. It is the Land of Hope and Glory. It is the hallelujahs of the saints, and the face of God. At the same time, it is only a lifeless, soulless, almost meaningless blur, though no doubt with infinite possibilities and potentialities. It is the stone which the builders rejected.

Taking an example from non-natural objects,—is beauty in the eye of the beholder, or in the picture? The Buddhist answer would be that it is in the eye, the mind. The Christian reply is that the beauty is in God, faintly reproduced in the picture, and dimly seen by us. The Zen view, and the right one, is that beauty exists when and only when I am the picture. Though the picture is a bad one, or even a blank canvas, there is still Zen, if and when I am the canvas, but beauty arises when the canvas has already suffered a sea-change, a universe-change, a Zen-change. That is to say, man is (also) a social animal, a solitary hive-bee. No man liveth to himself, (or to others) and the true half-history of the world is the history of the reunification of things (pictures) and man.

Mind is not produced by a mindless universe; it is involved in it from the very beginning, which "looks" forward to its end. The immortality of the soul was denied by primitive Buddhism, since the soul itself had no existence as an indivisible entity. Even now, at

ZEN AND CULTURE

Zen is culture, and culture is Zen, and that is all ye know on earth and all ye need to know,—if you also happen to know what what either Zen or culture is. What is culture?

The two Englishmen who have written most vitally, that is, most culturally about culture are Pater and Arnold. The latter's view is wider, the former's more intense. Arnold defines culture as "a pursuit of our total perfection by means of getting to know...the best which had been thought and said in the world; and through this knowledge, turning a stream of fresh and free thought upon our stock notions and habits."

There are three points to notice here. First, for culture, our own experience and the second-hand experience we derive from books etc. must be applied to our daily life and thought. Second, "total perfection" is a *harmonious* perfection of the individual, and a *general* perfection, his development as a social creature, a making the will of God to prevail on earth. Third, and most important, culture is not perfection; it is the pursuing of perfection; something that is moving and alive, not complete; not a having and a resting, but a growing and a becoming. What is essential is not the answer but the questions; the answers indeed are the death of the life that is in the questions.

Pater emphasizes, overemphasizes perhaps, the importance of the "moments of vision," the "spots of time." But when he says that the service of culture towards the human spirit is "to rouse, to startle it to a life of constant and eager observation," he points to its dynamic and continuous nature. He says further that "to burn always with this hard, gem-like flame, to maintain this ecstasy, is success in life." The hardness of this flame is directed against all that is less than perfect, that says what should not be said; anything over-refined; anything crude; whatever asks for pity or admiration.

In our cultural growth, as we move among the thoughts and experiences of East and West, one explains the other; they complement and illustrate each other by contrast. They delight us with their differences, and their secret inexpressible uniformities. We range from the animal intensity of the sculptures of Central Mexico to the transcendental calm of the Buddhist statues, from the tropical swamps of primaeval forests to the asphalt of Park Lane, and feel at home everywhere:

> All places that the eye of heaven visit
> Are to the wise man ports and happy havens.

Spengler declares that this is not so, that a man of one culture cannot understand another. He is right however, when he says that "practical requirements, so-called, are merely the mask of a profound inward compulsion," that is, of Zen. To take an example of this, New York has a great many sky-scrapers; why is this? The ordinary answer is, because land is scarce, and it is more convenient and cheaper to build upwards than to build outwards. Spengler's answer would be that this is an *excuse* hiding the real reason, which is a desire for infinity, for the vast and limitless. More simply, it is the expression of the American desire for the biggest, the highest, the superlative of everything. Another example is found in Stevenson's *Will O' The Mill*. Such great movements as the march of the barbarians towards the South and West of Europe, and the discovery of the New World are often ascribed to a desire for food and gold. Stevenson rightly calls this "a dull and pitiful explanation," and says that it was due to "the divine unrest" of humanity.

This leads us to another of Spengler's ideas, that culture is something that really lives only at the moment of creation by the author, (to a much lesser extent at the time of re-creation by the reader or listener,) so that what we usually call culture, books and sculptures, etc., are nothing but fossils, footprints on the shores of time after the traveller has passed. Spengler shows us the secret life, that is to say, the Zen that unites such different phenomena as differential calculus and the dynastic principle of politics of the age of Louis XIV; the Classical city state and Euclidean geometry; space perspective of Western oil-painting and the railroad, telephone and long-range weapons; contrapuntal music and credit economics. When we feel these deep uniformities, our culture becomes as vast as the history of the world; there is something god-like in it. We are able to range throughout the whole extent of things, and have a Shakespearean fellow-feeling for the intolerant or reactionary, and for those who have a blind desire for the mechanical and destructive; these latter will no doubt increase in number as the world grows older, as it nears that one far-off divine event which is the annihilation of all things.

Lawrence taught us that the intuitive and rational modes of apprehension are mutually exclusive, in other words, that we cannot enjoy the beauty of a thing and at the same time understand it intellectually, scientifically. This is no doubt true, but the intellect has a great value, albeit a negative one. First, it is not a coincidence that Buddha and Christ were both very clever men. Only those with a keen and trained intellect know how useless it is for the grasping of living truth. Second, though without faith (that is, poetry) we can do nothing, "it is our scepticism of mechanical fate that keeps the will free." Without the comparative intellect we cannot distinguish clearly false Zen from true Zen. A man becomes a monk, and after several years he gets satori, but what has happened to his common sense? Without common sense it is impossible to please God.

A more practical difficulty is the question how to act when our culture, that is our line of approach, our "standard" of judgement is opposed by parents, by society and public opinion. We are in a dilemma here, for if we fight for our opinions, they are debased, devitalized and petrified in the process; if we swim with the stream, at the best we shall be insincere, at the worst become conventional and lifeless. I know of no answer to this save to say that in actual life we are not hated for our virtues; we are not crucified for our goodness. The spitefulness and destructiveness latent in our hearts and hidden under our good intentions are perhaps the chief cause of persecution and opposition. Sometimes it is good to be like Will o' the Mill, a kind of living contradiction, "a talkative, inscrutable young man." When the worst comes, we may say with Confucius, Heaven knows me!

Thoreau's advice is, "Find out as soon as possible what are the best things in your composition, and then shape the rest to fit them. The former will be the midrib and veins of the leaf." From whatever region they come, these experiences are vivifying and direction-giving, or rather, direction-revealing. With them the pattern of a boy or girl's life is decided; the success or failure of their life then depends partly on circumstances, partly on what we call, rightly or wrongly, free-will. Culture is really the integration of these repeated moments of experience, so deep and unforgettable, and the daily round, the common task of ordinary life. Where these are separated, daily life is a grinding slavery in a prison house, and "culture" but concert-going, visiting museums, reading the "best books."

Culture, like Zen, is on the one hand something that is passed on from generation to generation. "A line of communication is established by which the flame of religious and civil liberty is kept alive." On the other hand, culture is individual; there is nothing imitative or second-hand about it. In this way we see how different education and culture are. It is surprising how much a man may know and not be cultured, how little learning he may have, and yet be living a life of poetry.

People speak much of Beauty, Goodness, and Truth, of Art, Morality, and Science, but these are not really culture, which is living in the life of *things*. The "life" of so-called inanimate things may be thought of as their essential existence, that by which they are what they are. Another way of viewing the matter is to understand that the cultured man, the poet, raises in power, in rank, in value, the various degrees of being: rocks, plants, animals, men, gods. So Wordsworth says that to

> Even the loose stones that cover the highway,
> I gave a moral life,

raising them up three grades of existence. Shelley says that the stars see themselves within the depths of the ocean:

> As the sharp stars pierce winter's crystal air,
> And gaze upon themselves within the sea.

Chaucer tells us that it is the nightingale "That clepeth forth the grene leves newe." Vaughan says that in the praise of God, poor stones are "deep in admiration." It is the superior energy of the poet that enables him to give more life to things than ordinary people credit them with; culture is this increasing of life, this life more abundant. Wordsworth says:

> And 'tis my faith that every flower
> Enjoys the air it breathes.

If we ask, "Is the moon really delighted?" "Do the flowers actually enjoy the air they breathe?" honest people say "No"; the cunning say, "It is *poetically* true," but this after all makes poetry a pretence, a deception, something that can never really and finally satisfy us. We must believe our intuitions, and say to every one of our rational objections, "By heaven, I'll make a ghost of him that lets me!" Not only in moral, but in poetical matters also,

> Tasks in hours of insight willed,
> May be in hours of gloom fulfilled;

and what was perceived in moments of excitement must
be recollected in tranquillity. When Shakespeare tells
us, of life,

> It is a tale
> Told by an idiot, full of sound and fury,
> Signifying nothing,

it is useless to point out that this is said by a murderer,
at a time of the failure of all his machinations. When
we read Macbeth's words we know immediately that
they are true; they are themselves their own proof.
While we read,

> The Lord is my Shepherd; I shall not want,

we cannot doubt it, for "Truth can never be told so
as to be understood, and not be believed."

Our chief duty is to strengthen our own feebleness,
to build up that pattern of life which destiny has decreed
for us. But at the same time we must say that the
highest test of culture, one which few indeed can pass,
is that of being able to understand and assimilate what
is by its nature foreign to us, that for which we have
but "imperfect sympathies." "Foreign" is not a matter
of time and place. When we read the poems of Haku-
rakuten, for example, we may feel more akin, nearer
spiritually and physically, than we do to our own father.
But there are moods alien to our own, not higher or
lower, but simply different, as a mole is from a hawk.
And these are needed, once our own line of life has
been established, to give it balance and roundness, for
after all our aim is perfection, a fullness and all-
inclusiveness. And what we cannot assimilate always
remains at least to disturb, and sometimes to ruin and
destroy us.

What is Zen? What is culture? In literature the
best examples come from Thoreau, for example in *A
Week on the Concord,* a past that is always present:

> As the bay-wing sang many a thousand years
> ago, so sang he tonight. In the beginning God heard
> his song and pronounced it good, and hence it has

endured. It reminded me of many a summer sunset, of many miles of gray rails, of many a rambling pasture, of the farm-house far in the fields, its milk-pans and well-sweep, and the cows coming home from the pasture.

The best, the most serene, is the present which is always present:

Autumnal mornings, when the feet of countless sparrows are heard like rain-drops on the roof by the boy who sleeps in the garret.

But besides the world of nature there is the world of man, and here Shakespeare stands supreme. With him we can look at a king and think of the pimp's words:

Truly sir, I am a poor fellow that would live.

When we see a beggar we can say with Kikaku:

乞食かな天地を著たる夏衣

The beggar!
He has Heaven and Earth
For his summer clothes.

Tolstoy, in *What is Art?* 1896, declares that what is incomprehensible to the majority of men is not real art. The indifference of the mass of people to aesthetic matters is more justified than many suppose. We wonder today at the profundity and beauty of Shakespeare's plays, written for a mixed Elizabethan audience. The *ukiyoe* of the 18th century were made for and sold to a public that now seems hardly to exist. I believe that this condition of affairs today is due not so much to the spoiling of popular taste by commercialism, as to the false values and dead artificiality of the high-brows. Lawrence speaks of those "directing all their subtle evil will against any positive living thing, masquerading as the ideal in order to poison the real." But after all, you can't fool all the people all the time; goodness, like murder, will out.

Humour is another quality, closely associated with paradox, that is both the test of culture and that very

culture. Bergson says: "The comic does not exist outside the pale of what is strictly human." This statement is either untrue or platitudinous. It is the latter
if we suppose, with the Buddhists, that "in the Three
Worlds, all is Mind," that is, everything which exists
is human. It is untrue if we distinguish the human
and the non-human, and do not remember the humour
that underlies and faintly tinges all haiku, however
objective they may be. A splendid example of culture
was given at a concert, when one of Beethoven's symphonies (I forget which) was played for the first time.
Between two of the movements, a man came on the
stage and played the violin upside-down, to the great
enjoyment of the listeners and Beethoven himself. The
"stodginess" of many so-called cultured people aroused
the fury of Nietzsche, and it may well be that a really
cultured man must have some irritability, some malice
and destructiveness, without which he would infallibly
sink to the level of the sheep and parrots that crowd
the salons and literary circles of the world. No doubt
we must have "sweetness and light," but also we need
nastiness and darkness, something rough and radical
in our character.

The enemies of culture are many; art for art's
sake, dilettantism; cynicism and facetiousness; ordinary
stupidity and superficiality; sensationalism; infatuation
with society, inability to be alone; lack of balance
between the new and the old; artistic snobbishness;
above all, sentimentality. Culture is on the one hand
the most delicate thing in the world; on the other hand
it is what enables a man to endure all the slings and
arrows of outrageous fortune. Nature has this same
delicacy and strength. The delicacy is sometimes too
great, as in Shelley, and we may "die of a rose In
aromatic pain." The strength is seen in the "heroic
virtue" of the muskrat, which gnaws its third leg off
when it is yet once again caught in the trap. It is
expressed in Wordsworth's lines:

> Stern was the face of nature; we rejoiced
> In that stern countenance; for our souls thence drew
> A feeling of their strength.

The strength also may be too great and fall into coarseness and insensibility; this is the parable in *Ruth, or the Influences of Nature.*

Has Zen any enemies? This question suggests that after all there may be some difference between Zen and culture. Vulgarity must be rejected by culture, but Zen means rejecting nothing, not even rejection. "Vulgarity" is perhaps the most difficult word in the language to define; it is almost equally difficult to illustrate, and this shows how near it is to culture itself. Heaven and hell are but a hair's breadth away from each other; there is no neutral ground. It may be said that the greatest writers have no vulgarity or sentimentality; they are not to be found in Homer or Shakespeare, in Milton or Wordsworth, in Bashō or Buson. In Goethe, Cervantes and Dante, however, I find some insensitiveness and cruelty at least. Nevertheless, one cannot say what vulgarity is, for it is vulgar to do so. It is not exactly insensitiveness or stupidity, for animals may have these, but they are never vulgar. It is in the will, in the choosing of what is low, loving the worse rather than the better, quantity than quality. We feel this vulgarity deeply and painfully, for it makes us doubt the ultimate goodness of the universe.

The relation of sex to culture is a profound one, and ranges from a man's relations to his family to what it decides, his cosmic attitude. The value, the life of a man is clear; poetry, art, music, science,—it is for the creation of these that he exists; but what is the value of a woman, what is her absolute value? Unless we understand this, at least unconsciously, our culture is one-sided, it omits half humanity. Even in writing these words, I feel myself to be addressing men rather than human beings. How do women feel when they read these man-made works, themselves as it were left on the fringe of life, "stretching out their hands to the

farther shore?" The value of a woman lies in her un-
yielding grasp of the relative. A man is continually
passing from the real to the ideal, from life to art, from
the relative to the absolute. A woman remains gladly
in her sphere, near to the secret heart of things, and
man comes back to her, to the bosom of nature, and
finds rest there.

Culture is the marriage of true minds, and the impediments of race, custom, language, place, and time
itself cannot be admitted. These true minds are those
that are not concerned so much with art as with life.
In Shakespeare, at least in his middle period, there is
an almost ideal balance between life and art. When
we come to Milton, the life is petrifying into convention,
the intuitions into figures of speech; we feel a premoni-
tion of the artificiality of the 18th century. It is
Wordsworth's great claim to fame that in his best poems
(and these are the shorter ones,) there is a minimum
of art, an aesthetic asceticism that goes farther and
deeper than the most eloquent of purple passages. For
example:

> No motion has she now, no force;
> She neither hears nor sees;
> Rolled round in earth's diurnal course
> With rocks and stones and trees.

The marriage of true minds is in this region, so full of
life that it seems to most people like death:

> Our finest relations are buried under a positive
> *depth* of silence, never to be revealed.

In Zen, all things are equal, unequally equal, equally
unequal. Enlightenment is illusion, illusion is enlightenment. Nothing is excluded, not even exclusion. The
more it changes, the more it is the same. The more
it is the same, the more it changes. Culture is the
deeply meaningful, the high-class, the unaffected, the
unhypocritical, the perfect. It is the best of Zen. In
Zen, everything is best:

> There is no great or small
> To the Soul that maketh all.

Browning follows Emerson: "Say not 'a small event'." Bach is Zen. Bach is culture. But boogie-woogie (whatever that may be) is also Zen, but not culture. Culture has the same character as poetry, described by Bradley in *Poetry for Poetry's Sake*:

> It is a spirit. It comes we know not whence. It will not speak at our bidding, nor answer in our language. It is not our servant. It is our master.

But Zen is not our master. Zen is the servant of any servant.

A fart is not culture. Even bottled, as the Romans did their tears, it could not be called "An Important Cultural Property," let alone "A National Treasure," even if it were King Alfred's. But a fart can be Zen, under two circumstances, which we may call active and passive. First, if the farter is for example in a drawing room, or in church, or at a museum, or in the universe, and, fully realising his true position there, and without fear or favour or exhibitionism or regret, farts. Second, if the listener, hearing the fart, and, while judging it to be either affected and impudent and malicious and vainglorious, or not, perceives it as a sound like any other sound (only a little more humorous than most.) We see then that anything may be Zen, but only some things can be culture; culture is always Zen, but Zen is not always culture. Zen is thus religion, culture is humanism. Culture is our making the will of God prevail, but the will of God always prevails anyway, and when we know both, there is Zen.

ZEN AND HUMOUR

When humour is at its deepest, when it is at one
and the same time the strength and the delicacy of
the humanness of human beings, it is Zen. When we
speak of the humour of Zen, we may restrict it to the
Zen (humour) of Japanese Buddhism. But by "Japanese Buddhism" we mean, "Buddhist Japanese," and
by "Japanese" we mean those people living in Japan
who laughed at and with the world. This laughter, or
rather, laughing, is Zen.

Religion teaches us how to "overcome the world,"
whether it be by submission as in Jōdo Shinshū, by
energy as in the Nichiren Sect, or by re-union with
the Divine as in Hinduism. Popular Buddhism, like
popular Christianity, is for cowards and fools like ourselves, and consists of escaping from this world to the
Western Paradise, or to a Heaven of some kind or other.
Humour, however, belongs very much to this world.
Life is suffering, as Sakyamuni pointed out long ago;
we cannot have what we want, and we must have what
we don't want, but humour is not escapist. It overcomes
the world, not by ascending into heaven, but by smil-
ing at the paradoxes of life. We overcome the world
by laughing at it; we overcome it in so far as we laugh
at it. Humour is thus a religion. It is religion itself.
It belongs to the will, to the subconscious will, and
sets its will against communism and democracy and
Buddhism and Christianity, and every other will, that
is, every other religion.

Buddhism, like Christianity, hates this world. The
world, the flesh, and the devil are lumped together in
the New Testament. In Buddhism the world is, as said
before, suffering, something we hate. Perversely,
Christianity and Buddhism both tell us to love what

we hate, to love our enemies, to be compassionate to the things or creatures or human beings that annoy and destroy us. Humour, on the other hand, makes us laugh at our enemies, and at our friends still more, laugh at God and the Devil, laugh at ourselves. To laugh is really to love. This we see in Hamlet and Ophelia, Othello and Desdemona, whose humourless love causes their tragedy.

If we take humour to be the nature of the universe, the origin of life and its object, the antagonism of Christianity and Buddhism to humour shows their irreligiousness. Of course, when we assert the importance of humour in this serious way, humour itself is absent, and we get only one more humourless -ism or -ology. What I really want to say is that it does not really matter whether a theory of life is good or bad, right or wrong, so long as it is humourously so.

The history of Christianity in England is the history of the addition of Anglo-Saxon humour to Jewish and late-Greek fanaticism and hero-worship. So, matrimonial quarrels were inserted in the story of Noah, sheep-stealing to the Nativity. People like Christ and Socrates and Buddha and Shelley have a mania, a megalomania for saving the world, teaching the unteachable. (So have I.) It is not possible to threaten, to frighten, to cajole, to shame people into Heaven. Can they be laughed or smiled into it? This is to some extent possible, humour being such a widely-spread thing, but the object must be, not Heaven, but laughter itself. Here, as everywhere, indirectness is best.

Coming now to Buddhism in particular, Buddhism was of course criticised in India. It was persecuted several times in China, for example between 438 and 452 A. D. by the Taoist To-pa Tao, and again in 845 by Wu Tsung. The famous prose writer Hanyu, d. 824, sent a petition to the Emperor Hsien in 820, begging that Buddhism should be proscribed:

> It is the barbarous religion, of which antiquity had no knowledge...of a man who disregarded his duties

as a son and a subject. And you allow to be pre-
sented to your Majesty a dry bone of that man, a
dirty piece of his corpse. Ah! I beg you to have this
bone sent to the executioner, that he may throw it
into the water or the fire.... And if the Buddha
learns of it and can do anything, well, let him revenge
himself on me, Hanyu, who will bear the full responsibility of your act.

In Japan, at the beginning of the 9th century, Shinto
and Buddhism were merged, but the Neo-Shintoism
of Motoori Norinaga and Hirata Atsutane was opposed
to the Indian ideals of celibacy and world-renunciation,
and chose rather the Chinese filial piety and loyalty
of Confucianism. However, what we want to know is
not so much the semi-official criticisms and professional
animadversions against Buddhism, but how the Japanese generally felt towards it. In this respect, the
proverbial sayings that have come from Buddhism are
extremely important, even more so than the personal
opinions of literary people in kyōka or senryu, since
they show us what the common people thought was
good or bad in Buddhism, in a word, what *interested*
them in it. There is of course a good deal of criticism
of Buddhism in the proverbs, for example:

Amida also shines with gold.

Buddha is power, and money is power, and so....

Outside, a Bodhisattva; inside a demon.

This is used of women, but may and should be applied
to nature.

A Buddha to worship, and a lavatory,—both
necessary !

Equally necessary.

The evil of Devadatta is the mercy of Avalokites-
vara;
The folly of Panthaka is the wisdom of Manjusri.

This saying comes in the Nō play *Sotoba Komachi*.
Devadatta committed all the Five Sins and fell into

Tanka (Tanhsia) Burning the Buddha, by Fūgai

The story upon which the picture is based is the following. One day, when Tanka, 738-824, was staying at Yerinji Temple in Changan, it was so cold he took one of the three Buddhas of the Buddhist Trinity in the Hall, and burned it to make a fire to warm himself. The monk in charge burst out, "What do you mean by burning my Buddha?" Tanka poked about in the ashes with his stick, and said, "I am burning it to get the sarira." [Sarira is an indestructible substance always (said to be) found in the ashes of a saint after cremation.] The monk said, "How should a wooden Buddha have any sarira?" Tanka said, "Well, there's no sarira so far, let's take the other two Buddhas, and burn them too!" The inscription says, 還我舍梨来, "Rather, I have the sarira."

Fūgai Mototaka, 1779-1847, belonged to the Soto branch of Zen. He became a monk at the age of nine, lived in various temples, and was a poetical and artistic person. The picture, painted when Fūgai was sixty one, shows us Tanka warning his posterior, the Buddha, as well he might, looking somewhat surprised at his unusual position.

Hell through trying to harm the Buddha. Panthaka (Handoku) was so foolish and forgetful that he could remember nothing the Buddha taught him. The above saying means that evil is good, illusion is enlightenment.

> The face of Yama-rajah when giving back;
> The face of Ksitigarbha when receiving.

Our very humanity, our Buddha-nature itself, requires us to do this, so that we may and should look smug when borrowing, and malignant when returning.

> Expounding the sutras before the Buddha.

This is what this book itself does.

> Trying to improve the Buddhist statue, and breaking its nose.

All improvement is really like this.

> My Buddha is holy.

Especially Christ and Buddha are not free from this illusion.

> The Nichiren prayer in the morning,
> The Shinshu prayer in the evening.

Namumyōhōrengekyō, with the beating of the drum, is suitable for the vigour of the morning, for young people. Namuamidabutsu suits the evening, with its quiet feeling; it is for old age. One more may be quoted from its similarity to something in the Old Testament.

> Dye your mind, rather than your garments.

In Joel II 13, we have: Rend your heart, and not your garments.

> Life is the treasure of treasures.

This is so, since without it no good is possible. This comes from the *Daichidoron,* a sastra, attributed to Nagarjuna, on the *Hannya Sutra.*

> Life is a dirty thing.

This is so, since to eat or to be eaten is equally odious.

Life is like a candle flickering in the wind.

But these flickering candles tease and torture and extinguish each other.

The desire for enlightenment is also illusion.

If so, the desire for illusion is perhaps enlightenment.

Look at the audience first, and then preach.

If we do this too carefully, we may never preach at all.

Religion also comes from greediness.

A desire for peace of mind, a desire to be desireless,— what a difficult world it is !

To faith, a lavatory broom also is the five hundred Arhats.

This sort of thing, even at its lowest,—the worship of the heathen who "bow down to stocks and stones,"— adumbrates the best, that is, the interpenetrative identity of all things.

The flourishing will decline;
Those who meet must part.

Is there no exception to this? No exception.

Small wisdom is a hindrance to salvation.

To Hell with moderation !

Zen, cleaning; Shingon, cooking; Monto, flowers; Hokke, offering; Jōdo, slovenly.

This seems to represent the opinion of the common man about the various sects. The first and the last, anyway, seem to me true.

When the temple is askew the sutras cannot be read properly.

We can't study in a tent. A good building is necessary.

Eating, and chanting the Buddha's name is bit by bit.

This is interesting as example of "physical law in the spiritual world."

> The one lamp of a poor man rather than the thousands of a rich one.

There is an exact parallel in the widow's mite.

> Hell also is a place to live in.

However painful our life is, it's our only life.

> A deaf man eaves-dropping.

This is a definition of a philosopher.

> Spitting at heaven.

It falls back onto our own face,—that is true, but let's spit anyway; it relieves the feelings.

> A hand-lantern and a temple-bell.

These two things look alike, yet are very different in weight. But looks are sometimes heavier than weight.

> Counting the treasures of next door.

All education is this, but it's better than counting nothing.

> A lotus flower in the mud.

This is one of the best similes, for enlightenment is illusion, since the lily *is* the mud.

> A life, even if you cry; a life, even if you laugh.

But a life without crying and laughter is not a life at all. Stoics, take heed!

> Those who chant the Buddha's name, and camellia trees,—is there a straight and upright one?

The answer is, as they say, in the negative.

> Poverty is the seed of salvation, riches the father of Karma.

This is something the world has forgotten, and may never remember again.

Buddhism and a straw thatch in the rain,—to hear them you must come outside.

This is a clever simile for the necessity of seeing the truth objectively as well as subjectively.

The moral (and even the legal) law exists because Buddhism exists.

What is chiefly wrong with society is the hiatus between the two laws. How can an ego-less judge condemn an ego-less criminal who has "stolen" what no one can really possess?

Worldly passion is, as it is, enlightenment.

This is perhaps the greatest paradox in the world, equal to the Christian incarnation, or the Hindu "You are not-you." It must have intrigued the Japanese from the moment it was imported.

Worldly passion is the dog of the house; it does not go away though you beat it. Enlightenment is the deer of the mountain; it does not come though you invite it.

These similes are good, too good.

Renouncing the world, but not renouncing oneself.

This is the fate of all hermits, whether scholarly or religious, so the only thing to do is to renounce renouncing the world, and then we shall renounce not renouncing ourselves.

This world is the accumulation of a thousand years.

This means what Blake said, more cheerfully: "A little flower is the labour of ages."

Life is short; the will is long.

Those who are satisfied with their three score years and ten are indeed pitiable creatures.

A potato-digging priest.

This gives us a picture of a priest of a small mountain

temple. It is a warm day; the priest is intent upon his potatoes; Buddhism is forgotten; the priest does not know that we are looking at him. There is a deep feeling of *lacrimae rerum,* until we remember that God is watching us just as we are watching the priest. Who is watching God?

A chestnut-bur priest.

This priest has renounced not only the world, but also all kindness and humanity, yet this has something consistent in it.

What the doctor gives up belongs to the priest.

And what the priest gives up belongs to God. And what....

A toad-eating priest.

The Japanese is "a sesame-grinding priest," since when turning the mortar to grind the seeds the body moves to and fro as if bowing to and flattering somebody.

A stingy priest.

It is odd that the Japanese for miser is *kechimbo,* as though the Japanese did not find out what a stingy person was really like until they saw some mean priests.

There are many popular songs, sung all over Japan, a great number being derogatory to priests. The following is an example from Yamashiro; it is a cradle song:

> The temple priest likes to gamble,
> Amida Nyorai he takes to
> The pawnshop,
> The pawnshop!

Here is one from Ise, a woodman's song:

> When Priest Saigyō was travelling throughout Japan, he forded the River Hosoya, and injured his foot on the backbone of an eel. Isn't there any good medicine for this? Yes, there are many: bamboo shoots at the end of the year; midwinter egg-plants;

mushrooms growing at the bottom of the sea; shell-
fish on the top of a mountain; snow in summer. Take
them in your hands, warm them in water, cool them
in the fire, knead them with the tears of ants, and
put the mixture on the wound, which will be cured
immediately.

Another example, a remarkably poetical one from Mino,
a children's song, shows some pity for the life of young
priests, who usually left their homes at a tender age:

A temple is seen through a clearing of the wood,
A lonely temple with one priestling.

The following is somewhat subtle, from Echigo province:

Ye...e...e...s! Day has dawned!
O priest who rings the temple bell,
By your favour, day has dawned.

This reminds us of Lyly's skylark,

The day not breaking till she sings.

Occasionally the criticisms of Buddhism are quite
profound, that is to say, humorous, that is to say, they
have some Zen in them, for example, a Buddhist Dance
Song from the province of Mutsu:

Something or other seems about to happen! Something or other seems about to happen! This dance
and that dance—let's dance a Jizō dance! Look at
Jizō dance! Jizō! Jizō! Why should Jizō be gnawed
by a rat? A rat is Jizō. If a rat is Jizō, why should
it be eaten by a cat? A cat is Jizō; then why should
it lose out to a dog? A dog is Jizō. If a dog is Jizō,
why should it be frightened of a wolf? A wolf is
Jizō; then why should it be burnt in a forest fire?
The forest fire is Jizō; then why should it be drunk
up by a man? A man is Jizō; then why should he
pray to Jizō? Jizō is Jizō. Look at the Jizō dance!
Look at the Jizō dance!

The most trenchant criticisms of Buddhism, that is
to say, the most humorous, come in senryu, satirical
verses written in the haiku form from the middle of the
eighteenth century (1765), and still being composed at

present day. The following are both ancient and modern.

> *Shinkō to   betsu ni ume ari   sakura ari*
>> Quite apart from our religion,
>> There are plum blossoms,
>> There are cherry blossoms.   Nanpoku

This is the double mistake, the mistake of religion, and the mistake of poetry.

> *Amari hare   -sugite sōshiki   chiisaku yuki*
>> The weather is too fine,
>> The funeral ceremony
>> Seems out of place.   Santaro

A funeral requires a rainy day, or at least an overcast sky.

> *Kasōba no   kemuri mo haru wa   nodoka nari*
>> The smoke from the crematorium too
>> Looks serene and calm
>> In spring.

There is no "pathetic fallacy" in senryu, and where would religion be without it?

> *Shinjin de   mireba sakura wa   chiru bakari*
>> Seen by the eye of faith
>> The cherry blossoms
>> Are always about to fall.

Religion is too prone to look only on the gloomy side of things.

> *Shinigao de   yatto ningen   -rashiku nari*
>> At last,
>> With his dead face
>> He looks like a man.   Kenkabō

Perhaps Kenkabō is speaking cynically, but inadvertently at least this verse justifies the Buddhist doctrine of the Buddha nature. Underneath all the greediness and vindictiveness and vulgarity of his life-long face there always lay the humanity at last revealed by death.

Unkei wa   hotoke no kuzu de   meshi wo taki

>> Unkei boiled rice
>>> With the shavings
>> Of Buddhas.

Unkei was a famous 12th and 13th century sculptor. This verse seems to have been written ironically, but also has a symbolical meaning.

Sekkyō ni   akubi mazari no   go shinkō

>> Preaching;
>>> Yawns
>> Mixed with belief.   Kanno

This is perhaps the true human nature, the nature of human truth, the true humanity of Nature.

Bōsan to   michizure to nari   satorisō

>> Happening to accompany
>>> A monk,
>> I feel near enlightenment.

So carrying a book under the arm gives us the illusion of learning something.

Zazendō   aita to miete   minna rusu

>> The Zazen Hall;
>>> Nobody there;
>> They must be tired of it.   Kenkabō

This is rather more valid than most criticisms of Zen, which are usually based on ignorance or misunderstanding. Zazen is not a means to an end; it is an end in itself; it is the end. Yet the Hall is deserted, as though the monks with enlightenment don't need to sit, and those without it are all right without it.

Iro otoko   de mo bōzu dake   yowami nari

>> A handsome man
>>> With a weak point,—
>> He's a monk.

This is an inversion of the usual way of looking at things. In *Makura no Sōshi* we get a different inversion;

The expounder of the Sutras should be handsome. We look fixedly at him and thus perceive the holiness of his teachings. If we look elsewhere, as a result of his ugliness, and don't listen, isn't this ugliness the cause of our sin?

> *Nii-ama no*   *ware to iyagaru*   *kagebōshi*
>
> The new nun
> Dislikes herself
> When she sees her shadow.

It is odd that the silhouette seems so much worse than the whole thing seen in the glass, but this verse belongs to a time when mirrors were rare.

> *Osho mukuchi*   *hanaseba zen ni*   *tesshi kiri*
>
> The priest
> Keeps his mouth shut,
> Or speaks of Zen only.

Mr. Blyth is like this; but this is not real Zen, which will talk of anything, even of Zen.

One aspect of humour is lacking in Japanese Zen, though not in Chinese Zen, and therefore in Japanese Buddhism, that is, pure nonsense. The *Mumonkan* is full of preposterous stories, which must have been popular in China long before "Shan" was ever heard of. It was the genius of the Chinese Zen monks of the 8th century which perceived the Zen latent in those stories, and laughed with their conscious minds as did the Chinese illiterates with their subconscious minds. But how can we laugh with our conscious minds? To do so is Zen.

What human beings seek for is a unifying principle in this apparently chaotic universe; and nonsense in one of them. The most common of these principles is science, which discovers (or creates) cause and effect. The trouble with science is that cause and effect are only too efficient as an explanation; there is no mystery, no wonder, no interest remaining. Another such principle is religion. Buddhism joins all things by giving them all the Buddha-nature, which "escalates" them somewhat mechanically to Buddhahood. Christianity marries the soul to Christ, who is one with God, but the rest of the creation seems to be omitted. According to Keats, Beauty is what makes everything meaningful,—but how about the ugly things, how about ourselves even? The hymn says love is "the tie that binds" things together, but the vast empty spaces of the universe do not look particularly loving. Poetry, in the practical sense understood by Bashō and Thoreau and Wordsworth, "seeing into the life of things," is the best so far, the "life" being the existence-meaning of things animate and inanimate. Humour also is a unifying principle, since it is possible, and even desirable, to laugh or at least smile, however grimly, at all things without exception.

The most remarkable, and most unexpected, of all these principles is nonsense. Nonsense does not mean no sense whatever; it implies a sense which is imperceptible by the reason, and can be assumed and justified only by an experience of that very "sense," that is, nonsense. There is a super-natural order, in which there is no intellect, no emotion, no beauty, no morality, no unifying principle, no order of any kind, natural or super-natural. This is the world of poetry, the world of Zen, of nonsense.

It is worthy of note that there is more nonsense verse, at least in English literature, than prose. The reason for this is that the rhythm, rhyme, alliteration, and so on, being themselves purely "nonsensical," help us to escape from the unreal world of common sense. An example of this is the following:

> Who killed Cock Robin?
>   I, said the Sparrow,
>   With my bow and arrow
> I killed Cock Robin.

Sherlock Holmes could never have found out who killed Cock Robin, nor could the most astute criminal psychologist, but the poet knows: it was the Sparrow.

How did he discover this? Because "Sparrow" rhymes
with "arrow." Why, at the end of the poem, did all the
birds of the air start a-sighing and a-sobbing? It was
not because they had sympathetic hearts, but because
sobbin' rhymes with Robin. And this, to a child,
Wordsworth's "Best Philosopher," is perfectly satisfying,
is perfectly clear. Compare this with the following
mondō.

> A monk one day said to Unmon, "A man may kill
> his father, and kill his mother, and repent before the
> Buddha; but if he kills a Buddha or a Patriarch, be-
> fore whom or what can he repent?" Unmon answered,
> "That is clear."

What is clear? It is clear that the question is not as
important as the monk thinks, that no question is really
important. It is clear that it is all right to repent before
somebody, or before nobody, or not to repent at all,
or to repent of repenting. It is "all right" as Browning
said, a little too complacently, for the sparrow to kill
Cock Robin. It is clear that everything is clear.

Nonsense sometimes consists of saying the obvious,
with pontific solemnity. We see it in the well-known
verse from "The Walrus and the Carpenter."

> The sea was wet as wet could be,
>   The sands were dry as dry.
> You could not see a cloud, because
>   No cloud was in the sky;
> No birds were flying overhead—
>   There were no birds to fly.

This corresponds exactly to the Zen saying, "The
flowers are red, the willow is green." It is in nursery
rhymes and ancient nonsense verses that we see the
Zen of nonsense and the nonsense of Zen at its best,
its freshest and most natural. In Edward Lear and
Lewis Carroll, as in much of the *Mumonkan* and
Hekiganroku, we get a conscious resistance to sense, an
intellectual defiance of intellect:

There was an Old Man who said, "Hush!
I perceive a young bird in this bush!"
    When they said, "Is it small?"
    He replied, "Not at all!
It is four times as big as the bush!"

The Thirty Eighth Case of the *Mumonkan* is this:

Goso said, "It's like a cow that passes by a window.
The head, the horns, the four feet all pass; why
doesn't the tail?"

The answer to this question is the same as that of the
March Hare when Alice asked why the two little girls
drew everything that begins with an M—. "Why not?"

Nonsense and Zen both make us free, free of emotion,
and intellectuality, and morality, and beauty and
ugliness. They enable us to escape from this unreal
world of egoism and competition and hope and despair
into the real world. Nonsense and Zen destroy false
sense, all sense, all science and common sense, with
which the newspapers and schools are filled. Above
all they keep us young and healthy. "Some nonsense
a day keeps the machine away." "Unless ye become
as little nit-wits...."

ZEN AND REASON

Zen is said to transcend logic, and this is very convenient for those who have neither, but logic is as human, as divine as Zen is, and it is not correct to say even that their spheres are different. Logic excludes Zen, but Zen must include logic. Logic is infallible. God is logic. When therefore the "conclusion" of Zen disagrees with the conclusion of a syllogism, we are not to deny the validity of reasoning. Rather, we are to request Zen to review its satori, or at least the expression of its intuitions, for satori and intuition are more quantitively than qualitatively different. To take an example. "I have enlightenment, you have not. But I am you. Therefore you have enlightenment." What has happened is clearly that the major and the minor premise contradict each other, and so the conclusion is invalid, as seen by the fact that it contradicts the major premise. (There are actually two syllogisms here, but they are jumbled together for the sake of convenience.) We should not however suppose that experience (I am I) and experience (I am you) are beyond logic. When we are speaking poetically, we are using words, like "tree," and "stone," which are not in the dictionary. "Tree" is a contraction of "Wordsworth's single tree" and "stone" of "Thoreau's old gray stone," and "frog" of "Bashō's adjectiveless frog." In the same way, in "I have enlightenment," if a Zen statement, "I" means "I-you," or "I-not-I"; "have" means "have-not-have"; "enlightenment" means "enlightenment-illusion." Or we may say, "Enlightenment is (real) enlightenment just because it is non-enlightenment (illusion)," and this is sufficiently cryptic to cause the hearer or reader to realise that the terms are not the dictionary ones. The fact is that Zen should use

its own language and never use that of the dichotomous
dictionary or the grudging grammarian.

As said before, words are the daughters of earth, but
logic is a Son of Heaven. If now we write our syllogism
in more Zenlike but uncouth and unpoetical and therefore not really Zen words, we get this: I-you have-
not-have enlightenment-illusion; you-I have-not have;
I-you am-not-am you-I. As we see, no conclusion is
here possible, because any conclusion is already contained in each premise, and each premise in the other.
But formal logic is actually no different. All men are
mortal; Socrates was a man; therefore Socrates died.
Here also the conclusion is contained in both premises,
and "All men are mortal," "Socrates was a man," when
analyzed, are found to be identical statements. It is
this nonsensical redundancy which Zen makes fun of
in "The flowers are red; the willow is green," and the
object of this statement is to make us realise that, also,
"The flowers are not red, nor the willow green."
Nothing is either red or green, but thinking makes it
so; even a poor philosopher like Hamlet knew this.

It is our nature to see half-facts: the stream is
flowing, the bridge is motionless. We live by half-
facts, and we die of them. But we are sometimes
aware of the other half: the bridge is flowing, the
stream is motionless. Real life, a full life, a whole life
consists in knowing, that is, experiencing the whole
fact. Then we may say "All things in Heaven and
Earth are full of beauty," or better, "In Heaven and
Earth there is not a thing of beauty." Both statements
mean exactly the same, because they are Zen statements. There is no contradiction, no fallacy, if and
when they are said or written of Zen by Zen.

The problem is how to distinguish Zen statements
from ordinary ones. It is said that it takes two to make
a quarrel, but one is enough for Zen, the speaker or
the hearer. Every statement may be heard as Zen, but
not every statement is spoken as Zen. In writing it is
sometimes convenient to use capitals and inverted

commas, though this soon becomes a trick of typography. "Tea which is (real) Tea is so because it is No-tea." This is a fact of experience, but there is a difference between tea and Tea, between no tea and No-tea. That is to say, tea+no tea=Tea=No-tea. But tea does not equal no tea. And perhaps it would be better expressed in this way: tea×no-tea=Tea=No-tea. Also, as stated above, though tea *drunk* may not equal no tea *drunk,* when tea is *seen* as Tea and no tea is *seen* as No-tea, then tea is no tea, just because tea= Tea=No-tea. We come back now to the original statement, about tea, which we may rewrite as: "Satori which is satori is so because it is mayoi."

A clear, logical mind is good, is indeed indispensable, not in itself, or because it leads to truth, but because it enables us to distinguish (a) enlightenment and illusion; (b) the world in which enlightenment and illusion are different things, and the world in which they are the same. But Zen is both worlds in one,— and yet not one. What will the clear logical mind make of this?

ZEN AND SOCIETY

The Zen Sect, and Zen priests, as part of general Buddhism, were formerly much concerned with society at large, and the various classes of that society. Especially during the Ashikaga Era, from about the middle of the 14th century to the end of the sixteenth, Zen monasteries were the libraries and schools and museums of Chinese and Japanese learning. Long before the Zen Sect was introduced into Japan, even in the seventh century, hospitals, bath-houses, herb-gardens were established, bridges were built, wells dug, canals for irrigation constructed, by the early Buddhists. Shōtoku Taishi, Gyōgi Bosatsu, and Kōbō Daishi are familiar names in this connection.

"By their fruits shall ye know them" is applicable in every sphere of human activity, and we must concede, though somewhat grudgingly, that the Zen Sect has conferred many and great benefits upon society. Grudgingly, because when we consider the relation between the Zen Sect and society from the political point of view (politics=power=money) we are far from satisfied. The Zen Sect has always been Vicar-of-Brayish, though so far with few Socialist affiliations, and this shows something wrong not only with the Sect, that is to say with the Chinese and Japanese, but with Zen itself (The same is true of Christianity and Buddhism. Not only the believers and founders but the dogmas themselves have something false, something unpoetical in them). When the Yüan conquered all China, the Zen organisation stated:

Our obligation to the Emperor is so vast and great that it cannot be expressed in words. To return this obligation we will certainly endeavour to realise our

48

Buddha nature and teach the holy doctrines to the people.

The Japanese attitude towards the state was equally subservient. Primitive Buddhism taught that kings and emperors were not to be flattered, and that religion was above the ruler. The Kamakura Military Government made use of mindless Zen to cut off people's heads in the most mindless manner, and to gain political ascendency by this headless means. It seems that Zen was most at home in the army, though it assisted the cultivation of the arts of peace as well. The relation of Zen to society is of two kinds, personal, and general, and the problems are therefore two. First, can Zen alter a man's character, and thereby change society? Second, is Zen capitalistic or socialistic, monarchic or republican? In regard to the first problem, we must ask a preliminary question, can a man's character change anyway? According to Shakespeare, it can and will, provided that the inner will to change is activated by outward circumstances. In *King Lear,* the only example of a man's change for the better (*Timon* is supposed to be for the worse) a selfish, arrogant, self-deceiving and sentimental old King becomes poor, lonely, and mad, and realises that this was his actual condition from the beginning, and the condition of all men for all time. This is his enlightenment, and by becoming empty of (the desire for) power (over others) he becomes full of (pure) power. Politically speaking, kingship is thus abolished by (the enlightenment of) the King himself. Others will take his place to the end of time, but few will abdicate. A real human being is one that can thus change, for it is better to be better than to be good. Zen improves a man's character by taking away ambition, if any; it removes evil by removing good; it makes men unselfish by showing them they are already unself-ish. To this extent Zen improves society, by improving the individual members of it. But what about the social system itself? As said before, Zen has always been on the side of the

big stick. This is its weakness, the desire to win, the
view that might is right. Morality is an odd thing. It
pops its head up unexpectedly, and love and beauty
and Zen and life itself must give way. Actually, Zen
should always have been on the side of resistance. It
was no doubt the absorption of Confucianism which
encouraged Chauvinism. But the question is, why did
Zen want to absorb Confucianism? The answer must
be the megalomania which attacks even the best of
men, Christ for example, and makes them believe that
their umbrella is God's umbrella, that my belief is *the*
belief and must succeed, and that therefore what
succeeds is my belief. This is the real basis of the
Japanese "love" of nature. Magna est veritas et
prevalebit. What prevails is right; my belief is right;
I am always on the winning side, the right side. But
the value of poetry (which after all is the real Zen)
is precisely that it is always on the losing side; Magna
est veritas et *non* prevalebit! There is no other way
to safeguard ourselves from the love of power over
the universe. Poetry is pure power; Zen is pure power.
It does not enable us to succeed; it enables us to see,
to see what succeeds, and to see what fails. After all,
blessedness (=pure power) has no connection with
happiness (=success) or with masochism (=the enjoyment of failure). It is just being a mirror of the glory
and misery of man, and crush of worlds.

Zen is somehow connected with poverty, not merely
the spiritual poverty of which Eckhart speaks, but
physical poverty, and it can feel little pleasure at
the welfare state envisaged by philanthropists and
meliorists. Shakespeare speaks of "the modesty of
nature," and this expression has also the modesty of
nature, but the modesty of Zen is still more modest.
A certain feeling of unworthiness, of unexpected and
undeserved joy at being born into this world, makes
us eat less, wear less, enjoy less than we might. In
some sense we are, unlike all the other creatures,
strangers and sojourners here. As Emerson says, we

always feel something missing in Nature, and this causes our ascetic modesty and diffidence. There are no "rights of man," no equality, fraternity, liberty, no vulgar "a man's a man for a' that." How modest is God? Let Christians answer this one.

The Zen State would be inhabited by people like Thoreau, and Thoreau's Zen means a friendly feeling to a friendly universe, not a sentimental feeling to an unsentimental one. The universe is friendly if we think it so, unfriendly if we think it so; which is it really? But what is the meaning of "really?" "Really" means deeply. "By their depth shall ye know them." The deeper always wins. Friendly is deeper than unfriendly, just as unfriendly is deeper than sentimental. Thoreau wanted "to think like a bream for a moment." The bream, like Hardy's insects, "knows earth-secrets that know not I." The aim of life is to know (remember) these earth-secrets, those of our fellow men, and particularly of our closest friends, who are the least known to us, and most mysterious.

In the ideal state, the Zen state, would all men be alike, or all different? The answer clearly is that they must be all alike, musical, artistic, poetical, loving, long-suffering. What then becomes of our kingly joy, the world not being full of such a number of things? First, the difference of the sexes is unalterable, until we go to heaven, where there is no Mr., Miss, or Mrs. Second, however long the world may last, such a state will never be attained. Third and best, all things are the same in eternity and different in eternity. Time is an illusion, but illusion is the only reality, and time is real. Thus the problem is only a factitious one, but at the same time it is a real one and will never be solved.

ZEN, SEX, AND LOVE

Zen is the infinite meaning which finite things have by virtue of their potential oneness with humanity, this "things" including the fifth leg of a horse, and the Middle of Next Week. Sex is the great driving power of the world; it is what causes men and women to re-unite physico-spiritually. It is part of the larger cosmic urge to join and to separate, the centripetal and centrifugal forces of the universe. Love has a three-fold character, Eros, Agape, and Philia. Eros is self-seeking, Agape self-renouncing, Philia mutually self-fulfilling. The combination of all three is the meaning of "God is love."

Zen and sex and love are similar, in their universality, unavoidability, and omnipotence. They are different, in that the aim of sex, or rather sexual intercourse is physical relief, but the aim of love is not psychical relief, except in so far as loneliness is unbearable. The aim of love is to love more, to be in closer and closer contact with the thing or person loved. The aim of sex is pleasure; the aim of love is blessedness; at the same time they are aimless, intrinsic value. Zen is aiming, when the aim is love or blessedness, that is, when there is no aim, no no-aim.

Modern psychology, psychology since Freud, has debunked love, and will soon debunk Zen; sex never needed debunking anyway. According to Reik, one of Freud's best disciples, love arises from envy, an envy which is the obverse of admiration. We "love" a person conceived as superior to ourselves, our "enemy," as a means of conquering him or her. This reduces love, both of and by man and God, to a mere egoism, but there is something fundamental and satisfying in this rational explanation which is lacking in religious rant

about love. Compare Reik's *Of Love and Lust* or
Schwarz's *The Psychology of Sex* with D'Arcy's *The
Mind and Heart of Love.* The latter is supposed to be
in praise of (Christian) love, but is so verbose that
nothing whatever remains in the mind or heart after
the book is read. The former, especially the first, are
almost cynical in tone, but leave us with a feeling of
the humanity of love and the love of humanity. Dis-
cussions of love fall easily into egoism, or pure
spirituality, or gush, or, worst of all, a kind of cold,
talkative, D'Arcy love which is really hatred. People
who love never speak of it,—and this goes for Christ
too. Zen feels miserable when it is spoken about, and
as for sex, "For God's sake hold your tongue and let
me...."

Religion makes love the origin of all things: "For
God (the same God as in Donne's verse) so loved
the world, that...." Science, that is, the science of
psychology sees sex as the gasoline of the vehicle of
life. Zen is the name we give to all the wordless words
and meaningless meanings and motionless movements
of our world,

> That *uncertain* Heaven received
> Into the bosom of the *steady* lake.

This Zen of Wordsworth is not devoid of sex or love,
as we see in the word "bosom." Yet when we look back
over the history of Zen, we find not so much an anti-
pathy to sex or a perversion of it such as we see in
(monastic) Christianity, but rather a sublime indifference to it. Women do not appear in the anecdotes
of the *Hekiganroku* or the *Mumonkan.* A book entitled
Zen for Women has yet to be published, and as far as
I am concerned is not yet in manuscript. What claim
can Zen possibly have to universality when it ignores
one half of humanity, and assumes sexlessness, that is
halflessness, in the other? There used to be much talk
of "sublimation," the transformation of the energy of
sex into some other form, for example aesthetic. But

this explanation begs the question here, which is, is sex a means, or an end? The Zen answer, and anyway the correct one, is that sex is, like all other "things," an end in itself. Sex, that is the body-mind experience, is value and needs no metamorphosis. Thus sublimation is no way of escape from the problem. We must say then that there is and always has been something wrong with Zen in this respect, not that sex is perverted or repressed in the life of Zen, but that there is something vital lacking in Zen, and something unnatural in its (apparently real) indifference to the life of sex and love.

It would be possible to say that the state of Zen is that of the mystical marriage of the individual soul to the Over-soul, the I to the not-I, and that satori is a kind of spiritual orgasm,—but somehow this kind of thing is disagreeable, not because sex is so, but because as so stated we feel strongly the disparateness of Zen and sex. Zen is freedom; sex is attachment and detachment in alternation, and true freedom is not even detachment. Shall we reject then the contentions of D. H. Lawrence and relegate sex to an inferior position? For him "human warmth," and "the right relation with a woman" were the all-important things, and after all, there is no warmth without sex, and Nature is our mother, not an incubating machine. We must never forget that the one thing in the world that is not a thing is Zen. International, transcendental, pure super-Zen has no existence. Buddha's Zen, and Daruma's Zen, and Enō's Zen and Rinzai's and Suzuki's and even perhaps Blyth's Zen, and certainly Mrs. Gamp's Zen, and the Wife of Bath's Zen,—but no Zen without them. Zen was produced, we say, in China, in other words and properer words, certain Chinese lived and moved and had their being in a way that we call Zen, a rather fish-like, loveless and sexless life. Fish-like Koreans and Japanese, and now Americans and Europeans are attracted to this Way of Life, a way that exists only in so far as there are travellers on it. The problem for us who are not fish-like, or wish we weren't, is—how shall we live a loving-sexual life of Zen? What is a sexual Zen? What is a loving Zen? These questions have yet to be answered in the experiences of living men and women; the answers must be "understood"; and they require further to be communicated from one person to another. Zen sex is like the other side of the moon, except that the latter is waiting to be discovered, the former to be created, if ever. A sexually loving Zen is like the Poor Thing in Stevenson's fable of that name, not yet a man, but brave part of him when the ring closes and the blows are going.

ZEN AND POETRY I

To write of love, or poetry, or Zen, or beauty has something disgusting about it,—and does this not already adumbrate something common in them, something indeed identical in a shadowy kind of way? Also, a discussion of the philosophy of Zen, the nature of poetry, the poetry of Nature, the sexual constitution of the universe, this is not unsurpassably difficult, but the question is, how much love has the writer in his heart, in his pen? How much Zen has he, that Zen which will not allow itself to be classified or exhibited or judged or identified or differentiated or indeed written about, no, and will not allow itself *not* to be written about !

When we write of science we must write scientifically; when we write of ice-cream, we must write ice-creamically; and so of beauty and poetry and Zen. Unless I have poetry and Zen in me as I write, it is useless to write about them, and if I have them in me it doesn't matter a brass button what I write about, in fact that subject of brass buttons would have been enough for Lamb to show how much Zen and poetry he had in him.

What is Zen? What is poetry? These are two questions that will never be answered, because they cannot really be asked. All such questions are asked by the mind which does not want to know, which wants *not* to know. They are what Coleridge calls "putting barricadoes or turnpikes upon the road to truth." But the desire to classify and separate and distinguish, to define, to limit the illimitable,—this is not the only form which the spirit of death takes. The wish to unify into one grand single principle is equally destructive of life and change and freedom. Science seeks one formula which will explain, that is, explain away, all the infinite variety of nature, but we also, we unscientific, yes, anti-scientific people wish to know all things as one, and one thing as the whole. And this is still the nay-saying spirit that wills to deny the differences in things, which reduces all to a cosmic stew of one flavour. Somehow we must escape from both scientific errors, that of analysis, and that of unification.   ,

Zen is what John Clare called English spelling, "an awkward squad." How about its relation to poetry, to morality, to beauty, to fools, to the ultimate annihilation of the world? Does Zen change a bull-fighter into a kindergarten teacher? Can Zen carve rotten wood? On the one hand Zen teaches us to follow Nature; on the other, to master it, to become The Master. We are to sleep when we are tired, eat when we are hungry; but at the same time not to feel "hot" in summer or "cold" in winter. Will Zen turn an ordinary man into a poetical one? As Wordsworth said, the poet has not only to reveal the object, but to give the eyes to see it with.

Going back to the bull-fighter: there seem to be two schools of thought. The orthodox says that Zen makes a bull-fighter, not *the* best bull-fighter, but *a* best bull-fighter, the best that that particular man is capable of being. The other view, which is my own, is that Zen will stop a bull-fighter from bull-fighting. What it will turn him into I don't quite know, but I trust my super-moral poetical instinct against that particular way of earning one's living (when others are possible; of course I would fight all the bulls in the universe to prevent my children from starving). That is to say, the Zen which only makes a bull-fighter into a better one seems to me false, or let us rather say, inadequately realised, second-hand, misunderstood. "God *will* (and I *will*) have all men to be saved from bull-fighting," and with God and Zen all things are possible. True Zen then must make people not hate animals, not wish to kill them, not rejoice in their violent or natural death. It must make one wish to reduce as much as possible the unnecessary, that is, the meaningless, that is, the Zen-less, unpoetical suffering in the world. To put the matter in an extreme form, no man has true Zen in him, no man has real *satori*, that is, poetry, who is not, or does not become, a vegetarian. Expressing it more mildly, to the extent that he does not actively reduce the amount of useless, fruitless pain in the world, to that extent a man's Zen is a swindle, a self-swindle, a Self-swindle. I am not saying, by the way, that there is anything "wrong" with bull-fighting. Of course it is something good. In my modest way I am simply saying that there are other, "better" ways of passing one's only life on this planet. "Better" means deeper, more meaningful, more poetical, more Zen-ful, with bigger and better bulls more gloriously killed.

I am afraid I have not carried my reader with me here, in dealing with poetry via morality. Let us take poetry more directly. Poetry is a meaningful activity, whether it appears visibly in walking or flying (in an aeroplane) or (bull-) fighting; or invisibly, as in thinking. The question what it means is not to be asked, or to speak more severely, the question itself arises from that secret desire we spoke of before, the will not to know, not to be. Poetry is the will to exist, the will of long things to be long, and soft things to be soft. This is the will to mean, the poetical activity *per se*. But coming closer to the ordinary usage of the word poetry, literature being poetry in verse or prose, we will now use the word poetry in the restricted meaning of literature in verse, that is to say, deep experiences expressed in rhythmical language, in repeated forms, for example the paralellisms of thought in Hebrew verse, or the repetitions of stress and line and stanza in modern European poetry. But what a violence of contrasts we observe even in the poetry of the same nation and the same age. The "faery lands forlorn" of Keats, and, "It was the first mild day of March," of Wordsworth; the lyrics of W.H. Davies, and Milton's "thoughts that wander through eternity." To go farther afield, the sensuous softness of Kalidasa, and the enraged sexuality of Catullus; the subdued mysticism of the Chinese poets and the lyrical masochism of Heine. What is the common element in all these? Can we call it "poetry"? Dare we call it Zen? Have we not bitten off more than we can chew? Is there anything poetical in Nansen's killing the kitten, or Unmon's putting his shoe on his head? The last question is not difficult to answer: these incidents are "infinitely" more poetical than the verses with which the *Hekiganroku* and *Mumonkan* are pedantically decorated. But this is too severe; take the most poetical line of the *Hekiganroku*:

> The sound of the rain-drops is heard in the empty hall.

This is Zen, and this is poetry.

"Poetry" is a term usually employed in connection with words; "musical thought," Carlyle called it. One of the mistakes of Zen is to assert that Zen is beyond thought, beyond words, wordless. This is like saying that no impression should be followed by an expression, which is the more foolish in that expression must always begin at the very moment of the commencement of impression. Words are not separate from things, any more than form is from matter or body from soul. This fact was well understood by the Shingon Sect. According to the Shingon Sect, more exactly, the Shingon Himitsu Shu, "The True Word Mystery Sect," there are Three Secrets, that of Activity, that of Word, and that of Meaning. The sect is called Shingon, "true word," to emphasize the underrated importance of the second of the Secrets. "In the Beginning was the Word," but just as the doctrine of the Trinity reunites the never-divided Father, Son, and Holy Ghost, so Activity, Word, and Meaning are in reality only one. That is to say poetry, most deeply considered, is the

True Word. Even when written down and printed in a book, it still lives in the same way and to the same degree that the man who spoke the words lived, and it is still living, and is insperable from him.

Poetry, like Zen, though incapable of definition, that is, of limitation, of isolation, can be exemplified. The trouble is, however, that what is shown is not necessarily what is seen, and *vice versa*. Nothing is foolproof (but then again, in case you are discouraged, nothing is sage-proof or saint-proof or poetry-proof or Zen-proof). Instead of defining Zen, and then defining poetry, and somehow or other twisting the definitions until they approximate, it may be better to point to a common element in both,—and this common element is perhaps we are all really looking for,—I refer to humour. The humour of Zen is almost too obvious, The *Mumonkan* in particular (and the *Hekiganroku* to a lesser degree because it is so garrulous) is simply a collection of cosmic jokes. Enlightenment is always accompanied by a kind of sublime laughter. It is an odd and significant thing that Zen began, or what is much more deeply true, is supposed to have begun, with a smile. Daruma in Japan has, quite properly, turned into a comical legless doll. We may think too of the story of the enlightenment of Shui-lao at the hands, or rather the foot, of his master Ma-tsu. He asked, "What is the meaning of Daruma's coming from the West?" Ma-tsu immediately gave him a kick in the chest, knocking him down. Shui-lao became enlightened, got up, and, clapping his hands, laughed aloud. Tai-hui tells us that when Shui-lao was asked what his enlightenment was, he answered, "Since the Master kicked me I have not been able to stop laughing." When Teng Yin-feng was about to die at Wutai, he said to the would-be mourners, "I have seen monks die sitting, and lying, but have any died standing?" "Yes, some," they replied. "How about upside-down?" "Never heard of such a thing!" Teng stood on his head and died.

It would be possible to give at great length examples of the various kinds of humour in Zen, of contradiction, anti-climax, practical jokes, Lear-like nonsense, inconsequence, impossibility, hyperbole, and so on. But it is more necessary to show how some kind of humour underlies all poetry, whether in prose or verse, painting or music.

To bring out the meaning of the word "humour" as used here, we may say that Mark Twain has little, if any, but that every sentence, even the saddest, of Thoreau's writings is impregnated with it. The real humour, like the real poetry and the real Zen, can never be separated from the whole, can never be pigeon-holed, can never become an illustrative anecdote. Herein lies the danger of such books as the *Hekiganroku* and the *Mumonkan* and magazine articles on Zen. By ceasing to be poetry, by being a collection of stories and essays they cease to have any Zen at all,—unless we can make these dry bones live.

The painful humour of *Don Quixote* is visible enough, often too much so, but is not that of *King Lear* equally easy to see? How terribly comical it is to watch Edmund tread out Gloucester's eyes with his heel! What a joke Lear's madness is! How fiendishly ingenious of God to kill Cordelia *before* he does Lear! Indeed the whole play is unbearably funny; it's a scream; it's enough to make a man die of laughing.

Admitting then that Zen and poetry overlap to some extent, let us ask the question, is there anything which is poetical but has no Zen in it? Are there some non-poetical elements in Zen? Zen may seem to be pragmatic and practical, but it is also wildly fantastic. It gives us the "sermons in stones and books in the running brooks," but it also has "magic casements opening on the foam of perilous seas forlorn." The words of Euripides are pure Zen: "At high tide the sea, they say, leaves a deep pool below the rock-shelf; in that clear place the women dip their water jars." But Zen also sees "the floor of heaven thick inlaid with patines

of bright gold," and hears the stars "still quiring to
the young-eyed cherubins." The enemies of poetry,—
vulgarity, sentimentality, romance, indifference, lack of
humour,—these are the enemies of Zen. Yet Zen, like
poetry, like humour, turns our stupidity into interest,
our falsity into a revelation of truth, our motiveless
malignity into meaningful "love," our defeat into
victory. Thus are confirmed the paradoxical words of
Socrates, "Think this certain, that to a good man no
evil can happen, either in life or in death." This "good
man" is the man of Zen, the man of Poetry.

ZEN AND POETRY II

Shinichi Hisamatsu, in his book *Zen to Bijutsu,*
referred to again in the essay, Zen in European Art,
tells us that Zen as seen in (Chinese and Japanese)
art has seven characteristics; all of these must be
present for the picture or pottery or statuary to be
called a Zen picture and so on. A Buddhist picture
has a Buddhist subject, but a Zen picture may have
any subject whatever, a mountain, two or three
persimmons, a poet-beggar,—anything will do provided
it is suffused with the spirit of Zen. The seven
characteristics of the spirit of Zen are as follows. First,
asymmetry; nonconformity in religion, lack of geo-
metricality in art. Second, *simplicity*; "Blessed are the
pure in heart," the omission of all insignificant irrelevant
details. Third, *agedness*; this is what we hear in
Mozart, not in Brahms; in the earlier not the later
Wordsworth; in Blake, for agedness means agelessness.
Fourth, *naturalness*; this is in some ways the most
difficult of all; how can art be natural? Is it natural
to die on a cross? Fifth, *latency*; this is the most
subjective of these seven characteristics; only the deep
can tell what is deep in the apparently shallow, can
see an infinite heaven in a puddle. Sixth, *unconventionality*; this is the democracy of Zen, in which there
are no kings and queens, no saints and angels, no
sacred objects and holy days. In art this means that
all subjects are equal; there is no "great subject"
any more than a "noble treatment." Seventh, *quietness*;
the mind, like the body, never changes its position from
the centre of gravity, that is the centre of the universe.
In art, quietness means, not that some peaceful scene
is portrayed, but that the lines and colours have a
common end and mutual assistance; they are not

hysterical or struggling meaninglessly with each other.

To these seven I have added four more, which are to apply to Eastern Zen and Eastern art as much as to their Western counterparts. They are, eight, *freedom*; no laws of morality or perspective; no adding or scraping off of paint, no repentance for sin; Nine, *humour*; the universe is a cosmic joke; the combination of opposites is the great law of art and life; not a happy ending, but a cheerful one. Ten, *sexuality*; this includes love and hate, kindness and cruelty, which are indeed sublimated, digested, but never transcended in the sense of being left behind. Lines rising and falling, entering, and being expelled, mountains and valleys. Eleven, *joy*; this is what every picture and statue must have whether it is of the birth of Christ or his death on the cross.

It will be easily seen that this classification is made in the Buddhist, the Indian manner, with overlappings and repetitions, which is again partly due to the fact that these are eleven aspects of a single thing which is itself an Aspect, something which God sees; and God is seeing.

Let us then resolve them into a smaller number, putting asymmetry, unconventionality, freedom and humour together under Humour; naturalness and simplicity and quietness under Naturalness. We then get Naturalness, Humour, Agedness, Latency, Sex, Freedom, and Joy, another and different seven characteristics of Zen in Eastern and Western art. What I now propose to do is to show that these seven qualities of Zen in life and Zen in art are equally applicable to poetry, to world poetry, which seems at first sight not only to have little connection with Zen but to be so heterogeneous in quality as hardly capable of the single name "poetry."

I myself think that Zen is poetry and poetry is Zen, but it is fruitless to quarrel about words. Somehow we must compare the Zen experience, the life of Zen, which is led up to by *satori*, enlightenment, quite apart from the various special techniques of Zen designed to bring this *satori* about,—and the poetic experience of poets of many places and times. This comparison is here to be made by showing that the Zen experience and the poetic experience have these seven characteristics in common, but this will not convince anybody. The most it can do is to confirm the experience of the sameness of the two experiences. This (rather intellectual) confirmation is necessary for us as human beings; at least we wish to know that what we believe is not unreasonable, not anti-reasonable, though super-reasonable it may well be. Thus we can preach only to the half or nearly converted. The unbelievers, the unpoetical, the so-called practical people, the scientists,—let them be anathema !

1

Thoreau says that poetry is a natural human fruit. "As naturally as the oak bears an acorn, and the vine a gourd, a man bears a poem, spoken or done." It is a great mistake to think of the words of a poem as signs or symbols of some invisible mental experience. This error is encouraged by the Zen Sect, which teaches "A special transmission outside the scriptures; no dependence upon words and letters; direct pointing to the soul of man; seeing into one's nature and the attainment of Buddhahood." This statement makes a false distinction, which Thoreau does not, between "spoken or done." After all, the finger does not point to the moon; the finger *is* the moon. The poetic experience is not wordless, any more than the soul is bodiless. In the original poetical experience the words are not yet separated from the experience. They are not yet printed in a book by a mechanical machine that takes us farther even from the first, undifferentiated state, perhaps a kind of primaeval will.

The naturalness of (good) poetry comes out clearly in its balance of form and matter. It seems possible, at first sight, to have a poor form for rich matter, and vice versa, but perhaps this is an illusion arising from the shallowness of our judgements. In theory at least, the profoundest words of Shakespeare have an equally (or even more) profound rhythm and sound. Strictly speaking a soundless, rhythmless intonationless word is as meaningless as a wordless rhythm, a mere / × × or a sigh or a groan. There is an old senryu, it is true, which says rightly enough:

いろいろと用たてられるせきばらい

Iro-iro to   yō taterareru   sekibarai

The cough
Is used
In many, many ways.

The differences of meaning however depend very much upon the circumstances of the case, and the persons coughed at, and we must try to hold fast to the truth that form is not the mere appearance of some abstract matter, but that form and matter are two different aspects of the same thing, just as "the soul is that portion of the soul perceived by the senses in this world." In other words, form and matter both derive from the (supposedly) formless, matterless, incoherent original experience.

Every thing may express anything; this is the fact that makes translation possible. This is the first great principle of (life and) art. When Shakespeare writes, or rather sings,

Full fathom five thy father lies,

we perceive that there is something f-ish about the universe, and also something th-ish, and l-ish, and [ai]-ish. So also in Coleridge's

The furrow followed free.

Though both are connected with water, it is a different experience that the f's express. In *Alice in Wonderland* the Dormouse tells us about the sisters who lived in a treacle-well and drew things beginning with an m. Wordsworth also says to his sister;

> My sister, ('tis a wish of mine)
> Now that our morning meal is done,
> Make haste, your morning task resign;
> Come forth and feel the sun.

These seven m's express some part of the love, "a universal birth," that is stealing from heart to heart on this first mild day of spring. But how about Hamlet's

> This is miching mallecho; it means mischief.

These are different m's, malignant, menacing, and malific. The same is true of rhythm. Iambs and trochees, anapaests and dactyls, not to speak of pyrrhics and spondees may express any things, any sounds, any states of mind. Trochees dance in *L'Allegro,* are solemn and heavy in Herbert's *Discipline,* are flippant in Addison's *Rosamund,* snarl in *Locksley Hall Sixty Years After,* are child-like in *Hiawatha,* and passionate and remorseful in, "Ae fond kiss, and then we sever !"

On the other hand, certain sounds and rhythms have a tendency (not to express, but) to be the audible and dynamic aspect of certain objects or emotions or profound apprehensions. The amphibrach, $\times/\times$, for example, is used in two of Shakespeare's songs, "Blow, blow thou winter wind," and "Under the Greenwood tree." In the latter, the line

> Come hither, come hither, come hither!

means, as far as the words are concerned, the calling of all those who are unambitious and love quietness to the woodland life, but as rhythm, it represents the merry note of the wild birds:

$$\times/\times \mid \times/\times \mid \times/\times$$

Alliteration, like rhyme, pleases by its suggestion of a secret unity amid all the confused and confusing phenomena of the world. Indeed, mere alliteration, without special (onomatopoetic) significance did this for Anglo-Saxon poetry, and it should be noted once more that alliteration is not really the suggestion of some underlying abstract unity of the universe but is itself an example of itself, that is,

> universal Nature, through her vast
> And crowded whole, an infinite paroquet,
> Repeats one note.

The repetition of rhyme, rhythm, consonance, assonance and so on, are eminently natural, but only when they are natural, that is, unforced. They are not completely spontaneous, for art can never have the higgledy-piggledy spontaneity of life.

2

It seems possible to write a history of English Literature with not a word about humour. Even World Literatures have been written with only a passing reference to it. This section proposes to show that not a line of good prose or poetry has been or can be written without it. The most subtle use of humour in poetry is in the opposition of poetic and scientific truth, both of which are equally "true," one however being living truth and the other dead truth. Things, apparently inanimate things, are either "alive" in some sense, as Wordsworth said, or they are dead in every sense, as science and common sense tell us.

> The moon doth with delight
> Look round her when the heavens are bare.

> Every flower enjoys the air it breathes.

> The river glideth at its own sweet will.

> The budding twigs spread out their fan
> To catch the breezy air;
> And I must think, do all I can,
> That there was pleasure there.

In these lines, with some diffidence and hesitation, Wordsworth tells us the only alternative to a mechanistic view of the world. Mechanical people think that the universe is a machine like themselves. The poet, full

of life and joy himself, sees it just so full of life and
joy. Which is "true"? It all depends upon oneself,
but it may be laid down that something is better than
nothing, and a machine is precisely nothing, whether
it is a cosmos (the flower) or the cosmos. We are
thus placed in a dilemma; either the world, including
ourselves is a meaningless chain of cause and effect,
or, daffodils dance, skies weep, stones shout hosannah,
and so on. Is a river flowing, H_2O+gravity,—or is it
"Thou wanderer thro' the woods"? The humour of the
whole business is the contradiction between the dead
truth of science and the living truth of poetry, between
the sense and use of ordinary life and the value and
uselessness of art. Literature is the struggle between
poetry and science, the struggle of life and death, death
in this case meaning nothingness, no-meaning.

Ruskin also dealt with this problem, and invented
the term "pathetic fallacy" to describe his defeatist
attitude. Objecting to Kingsley's "cruel, crawling
foam" he declares that foam is not cruel, neither does
it crawl, (foam is thus H_2O plus a mixture of oxygen
and nitrogen; together with the sea water it is affected
by the "pull" of the moon, and moves slowly over
the shore). The fact is that the foam is kind, and
cruel, and neither; it crawls cruelly and moves mindlessly.

Figures of speech are all jokes, indeed they are so
used in comic verse, but in serious verse also the
humour remains:

> So the two brothers and their murdered man
> Rode on towards fair Florence.

This prolepsis is as tragic and as humorous as the regret
of Shylock for the loss of his ring;

> I would have not given it for a wilderness of monkeys!

The hyperbole here is the humour which makes us
able to forgive Shylock his cruelty, thus half justified.
A. E. Housman asserted that all metaphors and similes

are mere ornaments, "things unessential to poetry." On
the contrary, poetry is nothing but metaphors and
similes, the one asserting a visible identity, the other
an underlying sameness. But a solemn metaphor is a
dead thing, and a humourless simile is hardly con-
ceivable. The metaphysical poets knew this, and,
overdoing the fantasy, rendered it ridiculous.

3

Just as comedy must include tragedy, so agedness
should have youth involved in it. Mere age is dryness
and a declining of life and energy. "Agedness" means
all of youth with none of its stupidity, insensitiveness,
egoism, and cruelty. It is age without its cynicism and
obstinacy and pride of power. What is wrong with
age is that it has no youth in it. What is wrong with
youth is that it has no age in it. Tichborne, executed
in 1586 at the age of twenty eight, tells us his age:

> I sought my death and found it in my womb,
> I looked for life and saw it was a shade,
> I trod the earth and knew it was my tomb,
> And now I die, and now I was but made;
> My glass is full, and now my glass is run,
> And now I live, and now my life is done.

In some ways drama, both comedy and tragedy, is
simply the record of the ageing, if possible, of the
characters concerned. We see it of course in *King
Lear*, but in *Othello* it is stated explicitly. He has
outgrown his boyish love of battle:

> Farewell the neighing steed, and the shrill trump,
> The spirit-stirring drum, th'ear-piercing fife,
> The royal banner, and all quality,
> Pride, pomp, and circumstance of glorious war!

In *Alice in Wonderland* we see the same ageing of
children, who still remain children, for example in
Jabberwocky, the perpetual delight of old children and
young sages:

'Twas brillig, and the slithy toves
　Did gyre and gimble in the wabe:
All mimsy were the borogoves,
　And the mome raths outgrabe.

4

Why should anything be hidden? Is it not a mere trick? Why much in little? Why not much in much? Is not understatement a kind of cowardice, or at best miserliness? It is no use talking about suggestiveness or imagination, for this begs the question, which is, why should we (be forced to) imagine what might just as well be displayed in full? When we eat Christmas pudding we are not asked to imagine the raisins.

The answer is that the question is based on a false conception of truth, which is not static and perfect, but dynamic and imperfect; it is growing, otherwise dead, and mere factual, scientific truth. Strictly speaking, the artist or the poet does not select the most significant part of the whole so that, in some miraculous way, the part may be greater than the whole. He chooses all that is living and moving and changing of the mixture of life and death in the object or circumstance. It is this living and growing of the "truth" of a thing which we refer to as its latency. It is its will, its existence-meaning.

As said before, a hippopotamus is more poetical than a butterfly, because its beauty is almost entirely latent. However, on a starlit night just rising above the water of an African jungle, the profound poetry, that is, the agedness of a hippopotamus is clearly visible. Lucy also had this latency, dwelling among the untrodden ways,

A Maid whom there were none to praise,
　And very few to love.

The incessant and nauseating praise of God reveals a latent hatred of Him.

5

There seems to be a great difference between Japanese and Chinese poets on the one hand and European poets on the other. Chinese poetry is devoid of romantic love; however, marital love and a sort of platonic(?) homosexuality are found. In Japan, some of the waka poets were, or pretended to be, Don Juans, for example Narihira, but the haiku poets seem quite sexless, both in their lives and in their writings. Without thinking of Sappho and Catullus and Goethe and Baudelaire, and confining ourselves to English poetry, the English poets were a pretty sexual bunch of people. Beowulf was quite a gentleman, but Chaucer was guilty, it seems, of rape. Shakespeare, unexpurgated, is not fit to be read in schools (see Eric Partridge's *Shakespeare's Bawdy*). Milton shows a strong interest in women everywhere, not least in his choice of Samson (and Delilah) as a subject in his old age. Wordsworth was always surrounded by women, had an illegitimate child, and probably was not guilty of incest with his sister. Keats' violent passion for a young lady with the suitable name of Brawne, Shelley's "feminated" life, and Byron's which stinks of women,—all these show that a poet must be a fully if not over-sexed person. The sexual respectability of both Tennyson and Browning is not unconnected with their dullness and verbosity.

If we make a comparison of the poetic form of Japanese (and to a lesser extent, Chinese) verse and that of Europe, we see the same difference. Japanese verse is in form excessively spiritual, almost mathematical, being alternations of five and seven syllables. European verse is far more physical; it dances with the trochaic and dactylic rhythms, or at least strides with the iambic. Poetry, dancing, music sex, religion, sacrifices (human and animal) eating, hunting, and so on,—these were once a single activity, and even now traces of the rest can be seen in poetry alone. Japanese and Chinese verse, even if connected with religion, is related to the pantheism and cosmic animism of the *Upanishads*, or the purification ceremonies of primitive Shintō. European poetry has blood, purgation, the agony of unfulfilled desire, Job's cursing of God. Sex and will are deeply related, at bottom the same thing perhaps. The most profound line of Shakespeare's plays is Lear's

> Never, never, never, never, never.

It expresses a despair beyond despair.

Lear's enlightenment, his realisation that pride of power is nonsense, is followed by Cordelia's death, by his realisation that what he loved had become nothing, and that the loving soul of Cordelia has been annihilated, is as if it had not been. But Sir Walter Raleigh has another "never":

> True love is a fire
> In the mind ever burning,
> Never sick, never old, never dead,
> From itself never turning.

Love and death have no connection with each other. One cannot have the victory over the other, for they exist in different worlds, one poetical, timeless, the other scientific, timeful. Lear's love, Cordelia's love are transcendental things, about which despair is impossible. There is yet one more "never" in English literature, the most tremendous of all. Blake says:

> And can he who smiles on all
> Hear the wren with sorrows small,
> Hear the small bird's grief & care,
> Hear the woes that infants bear,
>
> And not sit beside the nest,
> Pouring pity in their breast;
> And not sit the cradle near,
> Weeping tear on infant's tear;
>
> And not sit both night & day,
> Wiping all our tears away?
> O, no! never can it be!
> Never, never can it be!

This asserts the supremacy of the individual will over
all the apparent factuality of things. It is the final
sexual thrust, the masculine orgasm in which the
world is abolished. Nature exists no more to tantalise
us with her female charms. We have *Glad Day,* night-
less and sexless.

6

Freedom means freedom from emotion, from thought,
from beauty, from law, from self, from God. Does
anything remain? According to the Zen experience,
only when all these half-gods go do All Things remain,
does poetry remain. Art submits itself to law in order
that freedom may be brought out by contrast. Further,
it takes every advantage of (un)lucky accidents, turning its loss to glorious gain. When Wordsworth began
to write *To My Sister,* apparently in April, he said,

It is the first mild day of March.

Why this lie? Because "April" won't rhyme with
anything, and apparently there was a larch near the
house he had rented in Alfoxden. But also, by accident,
the sequence of vowels gives just the mood he was
in at the time. Also the m's of "mild" and "March"
have the same function as the six m's of the third
verse, the same function of love, "the spirit of the
season." The two l's coming together in "tall larch"
is also a lucky accident. They increase the height of
what is already high. Freedom thus means making
use of fixed fate, (really) liking what you do instead
of doing what you (think you) like.

7

Stevenson says that the first step to goodness is happiness, and joy is both the first and the last step to poetry.
Not that poetry has any connection with pleasure.
Indeed the function of poetry is to save the world from
meaningless pain, but no less, perhaps more, to save

it from meaningless pleasure. Pain has some hope of enlightenment, pleasure none. Joy then is Nirvana, is blessedness. In the *Dream of the Rood,* it says:

I saw then the Lord of Mankind hasten with great
   zeal
That He might be raised upon me.

This "zeal" is not different from "the deep power of joy" that Wordsworth speaks of in the *Tintern Abbey Ode.* It is not different from that of the "busy" orange tree that Herbert wished to be. This joy is not different (to go as far from happiness and comfort and self-satisfaction and success as possible) from those

Tears such as Angels weep,

that burst forth from the eyes of Satan when he surveyed the withered glory of those spirits who, though condemned forever now to have their lot in pain,

Yet faithful how they stood.

It is not different from the "luxury" that Thoreau felt when he cuddled down under a gray stone and hearkened to the siren song of the cricket.

Day and night seem henceforth but accidents, and the time is always a still eventide, and as the close of a happy day.

After all Zen is Zen. Humour is joy, and joy is sex, and sex is latent, and "age" is latent, and age comes naturally, and nature is joyful, and so the show goes on.

ZEN AND POETRY III

Zen is poetry and poetry is Zen. The word poetry, or poetical, may be used in three ways: verse, as opposed to prose; deep meaning in verse, that is Zen in words of regular rhythm; deep meaning, that is Zen, in verse or prose or sound or acts or states of mind. "Poetry" is used here with the second meaning.

From earliest times thinkers must have perceived that on the one hand they could not think without words; on the other hand, words expressed only half the whole truth. This experience may be verified logically. If a thing is all things, if each grain of sand is the universe, its sensuously perceived hardness, yellowness, smallness, lifelessness and so on must be accompanied by all the contrary qualities, softness, non-yellowness, bigness, liveliness, and so on, all equally present though invisible etc. to the senses. Words are thus as harmful as they are useful, and the early Zen monks naturally inveighed against the dichotomy of words. Literature became suspect, and this in a country, China, where letters and words and books and even paper, were regarded with a super-stitious awe. But it should be noted that literature, which is poetry in verse or prose, is no more and no less dichotomous than painting or music. A colour is every colour, a sound is every sound, a pyramid is a globe. Mozart could pick out a new theme when some-one was playing the piano downstairs, an oboist practising in the next room, a coloratura trilling from the attic:

> Carvers do not faces make,
> But that away which hid them there, do take.

Theoretically speaking, poetry, like all the other arts, attains its highest point when it says two things at

76

once, two opposite things. If these two contraries are expressed explicitly and intellectually we get a contradiction, at best a paradox, but the real fact of a thing is not a paradox, though the paradox is included, subsumed in it.

Zen is energy, the energy by which we rejoin what is separated, and separate what is joined. Zen is not tranquillity. Peace of mind is something we are always just going to have. If and when we actually have it, it has been attained by some insensitiveness, resignation, laziness, deathliness, stupidity, blindness, obstinacy, comfort-lovingness, self-satisfaction, emptiness. Poetry is the exact opposite of these. Tranquillity is there, but swallowed up in activity; the immovable must move:

> Sumer is icumen in;
> Lhude sing cucu !

"Come" means, has come from somewhere. Where is this mysterious "somewhere" from which all things come, and to which all things go? "Sing" is an order. Poetry is never indicative, but always imperative; it is our willing what nature wills. And here the poet of the 13th century is not telling the bird to do something it is not doing, but something it is, so that "sing" means "Don't stop singing," or as the poet himself says, "Ne swik thu naver nu !" Also, the word "cuckoo," in its imperative meaning (in haiku, most of the nouns are verbs; *furu-ike* is a verb, and *mizu no oto* is a verb) is the word, the bird, its voice, and its function (to be a cuckoo), that is, it is poetry.

Zen is found more in Fudō than in Kannon, in Hell than in Heaven. We feel it in Shinran's words in the *Tannishō:*

> I simply believe that we shall be saved by Buddha Amitabha when we call his name. I do not even know whether the calling of the name will take me to the Pure Land or Hell. Even if my teacher Hōnen is deceiving me, and I am sent to Hell by the calling of the name of Buddha Amitabha, I shall never regret calling his name. Those who have practised enough

to attain Buddhahood may regret calling his name
when they are sent to Hell and find that they were
deceived. But I am far from doing enough for the
attainment of Buddhahood. Hell may be my proper
residence.

There is more Zen in war than in peace, in cursing
than in blessing:

> Hark, the shrill outcries of the guilty wretches!
> Lively bright horror and amazing anguish
> Stare thro' their eyelids, while the living worm lies
>   Gnawing within them.

> Hopeless immortals, how they scream and shiver,
> While devils push them to the pit wide-yawning,
> Hideous and gloomy, to receive them headlong
>   Down to the centre!

The hideous and gloomy are as poetical as the beautiful
and severe, perhaps more so. It is interesting to look
through *The Golden Treasury,* or better still any
anthology of world poetry to find the Zen, if any, in
the verses. Old favourites become suspect, and other
poems, hitherto overlooked or disdained are seen to
have unsuspected value. Here are some lines from
A Little Treasury of World Poetry, 2600 B.C. to 1950,
edited by Herbert Greekmore. Whether there is really
any Zen in them, or whether you can put some into
them, Zen only knows.

> You are in me, and I am in you.
> Your qualities are my qualities.
>   *The Book of the Dead*

> Some eat the countries; these are kings;
> The doctors, those whom sickness stings;
> The merchants, those who buy their things
> And learned men, the fools.

> The married are the clergy's meat;
> The thieves devour the indiscreet;
> The flirts their eager lovers eat;
> And Labour eats us all.
>   *The Panchatantra*
>   c. 200 B.C.

I see a dog—no stone to shy at him;
   Yonder's a stone—no dog's in view:
There is your dog, here's stones to try at him—
   The king's dog ! what's a man to do?

Bhartrihari
c. 500 A.D.

The musk is in the deer, but it seeks it not within
   itself: it wanders in quest of grass.

Kabir
d. 1518

The rain has drubbed us in his cold laundry,
The sun has parched us blacker than a crow,
And kites have made each eye a cavity
And torn out beards and eyebrows even so.
There is no resting place where we may go,
But here or there, just as the wind may blow,
We dangle at his pleasure to and fro,
Pocked more by birds than thimble surfaces.
Be not therefore of our fraternity,
But pray God's mercy upon all of us.

Ballade of the Hanged Men, Villon

   The mountains skipped like rams,
   And the little hills like young sheep.

Tremble, thou earth, at the presence of the Lord,
At the presence of the God of Jacob,
Who turneth the hard rock into a standing water,
And the flint-stone into a springing well.

Psalm 114

For the stone shall cry out to the wall, and the
beam out of the timber shall answer it.

Habakkuk

   Yet a little sleep, a little slumber,
   A little folding of the hands to sleep.

Song of Songs

Now having washed and cleansed the robes of stain,
They spread them out in rows upon the shore,
Where most the breakers wash the pebbles clear,
Then the girls bathed and rubbed them well with oil,
And took their meal upon the river banks,
And waited for the clothes to dry in the sun.

The Odyssey

Tomorrow I will live the fool does say;
Today's itself too late: the wise lived yesterday.

Martial

Let, let the weary body
  Lie sunk in slumber deep,
The heart shall still remember
  Christ in its very sleep.

Prudentius

Frost shall freeze; fire melt wood;
Earth shall blossom; ice shall bridge,
Shall roof the waters, wondrously lock
Earth's budding growth. But One shall unbind
The fetters of frost, the Almighty God.
Winter shall pass, fair weather return,
The sun-hot summer, the restless sea.

Anglo-Saxon Gnomic Verses

TO MY COUNTRY

I've not sung of my country,
I've not praised its name
for the booty or glory
that battle yields;
just a tree—my hands planted
by Jordan's still waters,
just a path—I have traced
through the fields.

Very poor indeed—
I know it, Mother,
very poor indeed
is your daughter's offering:
just a shout of joy
when morning brightens,
just tears in secret
for your distress.

S. J. Kahn

One more example, to contrast with this, poetry of
the third kind, for it is in prose, from *Mr. Jonathan
Wild*:

But though envy was, through fear, obliged to join
the general voice in applause on this occasion, there
were not wanting some who maligned this completion
of glory, which was now about to be fulfilled to our
hero, and endeavoured to prevent it by knocking him

on the head as he stood under the tree, while the
ordinary was performing his last office. They therefore began to batter the cart with stones, brick-bats,
dirt, and all manner of mischievous weapons, some
of which, erroneously playing on the robes of the
ecclesiastic, made him so expeditious in his repetition,
that with wonderful alacrity he had ended almost in
an instant, and conveyed himself into a place of safety
in a hackney-coach, where he waited the conclusion
with a temper of mind described in these verses:

> Suave mari magno, turbantibus acquora ventis,
> E terra alterius magnum spectare laborem.

We must not, however, omit one circumstance, as
it serves to shew the most admirable conservation of
character in our hero to his last moment, which was,
that whilst the ordinary was busy in his ejaculations,
Wild, in the midst of the shower of stones, etc., which
played upon him, applied his hands to the parson's
pocket, and emptied it of his bottle-screw, which he
carried out of the world in his hand.

The ordinary being now descended from the cart,
Wild had just opportunity to cast his eyes around the
crowd, and to give them a hearty curse, when immediately the horses moved on, and with universal
applause our hero swung out of this world.

What is the common element in all these lines? It
is the nature of things, which is speaking with the voice
of a man, the thingness of things in Homer, the deathliness of life in Villon, the liveliness of death in Fielding,
the life of apparently lifeless things in Hebrew poetry,
the eating eatability of things in the *Panchatantra*, the
(thrilling because unexpected) mysticism of Ancient
Egypt. But the poetry of poetry, the Zen of Zen is
when the words and the ideas are undivided and indivisible (though a word has its own intrinsic value);
when you just can't explain why it is poetry, why it is
Zen (but you do). A poet is a mountain speaking
mountainously (not monotonously) of mountains to
mountains, just as Shakespeare is a Hamlet speaking
Hamletically of Hamlets to Hamlets. But when we
say this kind of thing, or when we say "This is Zen;
this is poetry; poetry is Zen," everything is spoiled.

ZEN AND SHELLEY

Shelley's love of the indefinite, the infinite, and his excessive horror of "man's inhumanity to man," give us an impression of a lack of Zen which the high quality and comprehensive range of his poetic work contradicts. On the one hand he is "Dizzy, lost, but unbewailing"; on the other, he says he loves

> Everything almost
> Which is Nature's and may be
> Untainted by man's misery.

"Almost" is a strange word for Shelley to use. But he goes farther than this, when he says of the poet, that is, of himself:

> He will watch from dawn to gloom
> The lake-reflected sun illume
> The yellow bees in the ivy bloom,
> Nor heed nor see what things they be,
> But from these create he can
> Forms more real than living man,
> Nurslings of immortality![1]

For a man to cut himself off from ordinary life, "Nor seeks nor finds he mortal blisses," seems far indeed from the practicality, the materialism of Zen, at least as developed in Japan. It corresponds perhaps to the Indian or early Chinese period of Zen.

The effect of Shelley's intense preoccupation with the abstract is the same as that of Keats in the *Nightingale Ode*. When that light which alone can give value to "life's unquiet dream" is quenched, Shelley falters. "Spirit of Beauty...where art thou gone?" Yet, following Plato and his own experience of life, he knows that

---

1. *Prometheus Unbound*.

> The everlasting universe of things
> Flows through the mind,

that the mind of man is the Mind which moves the stars and upholds the mountains. So of Mt. Blanc he says:

> The secret strength of things
> Which governs thought, and to the infinite dome
> Of heaven is as a law, inhabits thee!

This "secret strength of things," which is Zen, is the source of all our life,

> Which drives them on their path, while they
> Believe their own swift wings and feet
> The sweet desires within obey.

This is a deep truth perverted into Calvinism.

Shelley could see and portray the outside world as well as any other great poet. The following well-known *Song* dates from 1822, the year of his death.

> A widow bird sat mourning for her love
> Upon a wintry bough;
> The frozen wind crept on above,
> The freezing stream below.
>
> There was no leaf upon the forest bare,
> No flower upon the ground,
> And little motion in the air
> Except the mill-wheel's sound.

This is the region of haiku, the thing as it is with nothing added, rather subtracted. (The first line is as purely ornithological as any text-book on birds and bird-life.) But the Zen of Shelley lies precisely where we would not expect to find it, in his love of the vague and vast, in the multitudinous images vanishing and reappearing, in a confusion which yet has a unifying principle of creative life within it. The world in which he lives is that of *The Cloud*:

> Like a child from the womb, like a ghost from the tomb,
> I arise and unbuild it again.

Zen would ask, "Who is this 'I'?" Speaking of himself
in *Adonais* Shelley says,

> And his own thoughts, along that rugged way,
> Pursued, like raging hounds, their father and their
> prey.

This change of mind that came naturally to Shelley,
this change that is so painful to ordinary people,
Shelley elevates into the very principle of living itself.
Echoing those famous words of the *Diamond Sutra,*

> Awaken the mind without fixing it anywhere,

he asserts,

> > Narrow
> The heart that loves, the brain that contemplates,
> The life that wears, the spirit that creates
> One object, and one form, and builds thereby
> A sepulchre for its eternity.[2]

His own personality is fluid, and his poetry flows from
his imagination and intellectual activity rather than
from his own individuality:[3]

> > The beams of the sunrise, flow in,
> Unimpeded, keen, golden, and crystalline,
> Banded armies of light and air.[4]

These lines, and the following, correspond to Turner's
Wind, Rain, and Steam, in their life and freedom:

> On the blue surface of thine airy surge
> Like the bright hair uplifted from the head
> Of some fierce Maenad, even from the dim verge
> Of the horizon to the zenith's height,
> The locks of the approaching storm.

In such passages we feel the divergence between Shelley
and Wordsworth. For Wordsworth, man is man and
Nature is Nature. In Shelley, man is Nature and

---

2. *Epipsychidion.*
3. Especially *The Witch of Atlas.*
4. *Vision of the Sea.*

Nature is man, sometimes, as in *Alastor,* in the sense
that Nature and man reflect each other, but more often
the Life of life is expressed, by which we see Nature
as impersonally as a scientist sees her, yet with Nature's
own powerful incalculability. In the *Ode to the West
Wind,* Shelley utters a prayer for what was granted
to him at birth:

> Be thou, spirit fierce,
> My spirit! Be thou me, impetuous one!

It is this spirit which breathes in the ardour of

> Gazing on thee I feel, I know,
> Green stalks burst forth and bright flowers grow,
> And living shapes upon my bosom move....
> It interpenetrates my granite mass,
> Through tangled roots and trodden clay doth pass,
> In the utmost leaves and delicatest flowers.[5]

There is the same élan in Bashō's verse:

> Oh, how glorious
> The young leaves, the green leaves,
> Glittering in the sunshine!

The Zen of Shelley's poetry may be considered under
two aspects. First, the skylark of *The Skylark,* is not
a bird but neither is it a Shelleyan creation;

> What thou art we know not.

Its unbodied Joy is not Shelley's joy. If it is neither
the actual, everyday skylark, nor Shelley's skylark,
what is it? Wordsworth humanises it, Shelley
dehumanises it; which is right? Both. On the one hand
the skylark lives life, and thus we may share it.
Wordsworth is thus right in implanting his own feelings within the breast of the skylark. On the other
hand, the skylark has its own absolute existence apart
from all other things. It is a Skylark; and Shelley, by
creating a skylark out of his own divinity, approximates

---

5. *Prometheus Unbound.*

to that skylark which God created out of his. As
Eckhart says,

> Darum nimmt auch der Mensch, der ungeschieden
> ist von allen Dingen, die Gottheit da, wo Gott die
> Gottheit selber nimmt.

Second, in spite of, or it may be because of his love
of the indefinite, the individual creations of Shelley,
for example the Cloud, the Moon, and the Earth in
Prometheus Unbound, Aretheusa, and so on, are not
mere waves of a great Sea of Being. Emerson's ever-
blessed One, Thomas Aquinus' God the Creator, merge
all separate existences into an Absolute. But in Shelley,
each has a separate, self-sufficient existence, quite beyond the reach of either pantheism or mysticism. They
have indeed the life of Zen, being neither in the
absolute, nor in the relative. This is how he addresses
them:

> Ye elemental Genii, who have homes
>   From man's high mind even to the central stone
> Of sullen lead; from Heaven's star-fretted domes
>   To the dull weed some worm battens on !

Chinese Zen perhaps arose from, it was probably
inspired, and certainly paralleled by the Taoism. the
transcendentalism of Chuangtse and Laotse, which
ultimately produced "elemental Genii." But the 8th
century Zen masters of China felt, rightly enough, that
mysticism was as much a danger to the good life as
Buddhist theology, and they emphasised the practice
of Zen in daily life as against supernaturalism as well
as philosophising and verbal explanation. Yet without
abstraction and generalities, principles and dogmas,
impossible ideals and ambitions, without, that is to say,
the chance and the ability to reject these things, a man
is not truly human. "Sell all thou hast !" is the
command, and this applies to thought and judgement,
idealisation, and the perception of truth, and goodness,
and beauty. Only a rich man can become truly poor.
Only an adult can be as a little child. There are no

children in the Kingdom of Heaven.

The Zen of Shelley consists not in his giving up the abstract and taking over the concrete, not in coming down to earth and absorbing himself into the particular man or woman or tree or stone, but in making the impersonal still more impersonal, putting yet more life into apparently lifeless things. Zen is to stand still while moving, to move while standing still, but there has always been too much emphasis on the standing still, the sitting still. Shelley rectifies the balance, by moving at all costs, too often at the cost of balance and steadiness, but after all, of the two, movement is better than no-movement. That is why God created the world. At least, He has no better excuse to give.

What is especial about Shelley's Zen is of course what is peculiar to Shelley himself, that in spite of his v-neck there is nothing feminine in him. He is like Thoreau, a man, in his love of truth, transcendentalism, and desire to reform the world. Thus Shelley's Zen is masculine, occidental. Chinese Zen was, and Japanese Zen also, for all its Bushidō, womanlike Zen, in its unintellectuality, practicality, conservatism, superstition, unteachability, self-satisfaction, love of ritual and fancy costumes, and, except in very special cases, no sense of humour. Shelley's Zen is the future Zen of the West, which will lack, as Shelley's did, the earthiness, the blindness, the may-thy-will-be-done-ness, the finality, the tranquility of the Zen of the East.

ZEN AND GRAMMAR

One of the most depressing experiences of my life was trying to read Jespersen's *The Philosophy of Grammar*. What a dusty answer gets the soul here to questions such as, why have things names? What activity is expressed by the verb "to be"? How can a part of speech be used as another? What is the difference between "All A is all B" and "All B is all A"? How does a preposition "govern" a noun? What is language? What is the relation between words and things? What language does God speak? Let us see what Zen can do for us. By Zen here is hardly meant conventional, historical, orthodox, patriarchal Zen, which pretends to view words as entanglements of the soul and the obstructing debris of the mind. Emerson has more real Zen than they: "Words and deeds are indifferent modes of the divine activity." As to the question of the relation of words and deeds, or words and things, it is clear that they are, or rather may be, two aspects of one thing. When words are the verbal aspect of reality, corresponding to the sense or mental aspects we get poetry, which is thus always a kind of onomatopoeia. Any real speech is always poetry, in words; poetry is the only real speech; what is wrong with words, especially written words, is that the half-truth of the separateness of things is over-emphasised, and the half-truth of the oneness of things is under-emphasised, as in concrete nouns, or vice-versa, in abstract nouns.

There are parts of speech, figures of speech; where is the speech? The chief culprit in this matter is no doubt prepositions, and particularly "of." In fact we may say that there is a universal mental disease we could call "ofness," with which we become infected at an early age:

I then my Bliss did, when my silence, break.

We are taught to speak of "the colour of the chalk," by which we suppose, rightly enough, that the chalk and its colour are two different things. What we forget, at last, is that the chalk and its colour are two inseparable things, separable in language and thought, inseparable in silence and intuition. We ask "What is the meaning of that?" Things mean, and things have a meaning, but even when we say "Things mean," the noun and the verb separate, in our minds, the thing from its isness, its activity. Even if we say, as we can in German, "A thing things," or as in English, "A flower flowers," or "A teacher teaches," noun and verb, however cognate or identical in connotation, deprive us of the experience, as well as the power to express it, that a thing has no meaning other than its own infinite one.

Pronouns, particularly he, she, it, are baneful. Poetry has no it, only he and she. All things are alive, as Vaughan and Wordsworth told us again, and have sex, as Freud and D. H. Lawrence reminded us. "It" is a machine, if there really is such a thing. As said before, prepositions are mortally dangerous, for example "in." "To see a world in a grain of sand,"—has this "in" the physical or the spiritual meaning? It should be taken physically, and then we get the Tendai philosophy of "All in one, one in All," but most people take "in" to mean "by means of," "taking (a grain of sand) as a symbol." It is necessary always to understand poetry and religion literally, not literarily. Perhaps the most important preposition is "like," because this involves simile, a weakened form of metaphor, which is an experience of identity of different things, the more different the better.

Interjections were no doubt the earliest form of speech, in being so close to the feeling of which they are a kind of prolongation. It should be noted here that the word "express" is one of the most useful and misleading words in any language. One thing does not

express another. A thing does not express even itself;
it just is itself. So the words "Blast it!" does not
express a feeling of impotent anger. It is part, a potent
part, of the impotence of the anger. Without the exclamation there is no anger; without anger there is no
(real) exclamation. Thus a word is real in far as it
is part of a thing. A thing is not real until it has its
own word. We make things real with words; real
things are things speaking. We make words real in
so far as they are things in sound, not so much the
sound of things as things sounding.

In poetry, especially in Japanese poetry, there are
no nouns, only verbs. So for example in the too famous
verse:

> The old pond!
> A frog-jumps-in sound
> Of the water.

"A frog jumps in" is not a clause but an adjectival
phrase qualifying "sound." "Pond" is, poetically, vitally
speaking, a verb; "sound of the water" is a verb. In
the beginning was the Verb, not the Noun, the active
and creative Word, not the passive and created Word.
When Oliver Twist asked for more, "more" was a verb;
it was the French Revolution and the Russian Revolution. "But me no buts!" or "Humph!" is language
at its most powerful. In the Chinese language there is
no distinction of parts of speech, and the concrete and
vivid power of the Chinese characters makes it clear
that 木 is not merely a tree, but a tree growing, a tree
treeing; 火 is not so much "(There is a) fire," as "(I
am) burning!" 泪 is not water in the eye, but an eye
weeping, or water eyeing. In this sense Chinese,
especially written Chinese, must be called the best of
all languages, just as it is the best for Zen, and if ever
the Japanese or the Chinese give up their hieroglyphics,
they will give up most of their culture with them.

We must suppose that in the order of time, verbs, in
their exclamatory, imperative form, arose first. To
primitive man the outside world expanded and con-

tracted, thrust itself upon him or escaped at every
turn; he imagined all these things, he imagined his
world, and his world imagined him. At this time, things
spoke to him in their often silent language and he
spoke to them in his, which was also often silent, in
the beating of his blood and the expanding nostrils
and clenched first. He began to imagine himself
separate from outside things, just as he had imagined
himself one with them and would one day feel home-
sick for that unity. Now language is to come into
existence. There are no words separate from himself,
no sounds separate from things. Nature is always
speaking, with sounds or by other means, himself also.
Each man now gradually becomes more and more
isolated, in his hopes and fears, hungers and satisfac-
tions, from his fellows. But the falling waters have the
same familiar or ominous voice, and the men around
him make the same zoo-like, school-playground-like
noises. Men are joined, are re-joined by language.
Later, language itself becomes separate, and you might
even fell a man with Webster's Dictionary, if you could
lift it. To join, to separate, to re-join, to re-separate,—
this sexual, centripetal centrifugality is the essence of
life, the essence of Zen. A word is a (real) word because it is not a word, because it is a thing, a thing
which is a real thing only when it is not a thing, when
it is a word. The charm of language, that charm without which, as Emerson says, nothing can conquer me,
consists precisely in its separate-inseparate character.
In the Shingon Sect the separateness, the intrinsic power
of words is declared. The Jōdo Sect also rides us safely
to Paradise on the word *Namuamidabutsu.* In the Zen
Sect words are publicly denounced as being, like men
themselves, "deceivers ever," but the truth is that both
are right. The Word, the Logos is God, and yet not
God. Grammar and syntax are like the ponderous
tomes of theology that Hazlitt's father used to read
during the winters in his remote parish; they are
"comparatively a dream, but a dream of infinity and

eternity, of death, the resurrection, and a judgement to come."

Perhaps something should be added here about figures of speech, formerly relegated to the last pages of grammar books. Similes point from a distance to the sameness of things, while their separateness is stressed by the use of the word "as," or "like." In metaphors, the identity of totally different things is asserted, but this, however true and novel it may be, is often felt to be too strong, too one-sided, and is frequently modified by such words as "almost," "it seemed," and so on; an example from Dorothy Wordsworth's *Journal*:

The tree almost roared, and the ground seemed in motion with the multitude of dancing leaves.

Personification is perhaps a misnomer. If a thing is only a thing, it can't be made into a person even by the most zealous imagination, without a loss of rationality and common sense. Poetry is not pretending; it is the highest fact, and "personification," which means realising that every thing is a person, is an unnecessary word like "natural," for what can be unnatural? However, it is possible for human beings to depersonalise things, and the tendency of the world, withstood so manfully by D. H. Lawrence, is to depersonalise also persons.

Synechdoche and metonomy, taking a part for the whole or the whole for the part, is very Zen. We may ask here, why is the part greater than the whole? It is not that the part leaves something for the imagination to supply, but that imperfection is always better than perfection, and this is since it allows of movement and change. The changing and the changeless are both good, but change is better. So with the One and the Many. People with good taste love the Many, not the One.

We must look for Zen in the most unlikely places, or rather, in the least likely. Grammar is one of these, and, however great the effort needed, we must see Zen not only in criminality, ugliness, destructiveness, stupidity, snobbery, hypocrisy, affectation, sentimentality, and vulgarity, but, what is most difficult of all, see it in rules of syntax, mechanicality, automation, pure nothingness and sterility, in cant and rant, in essays on Zen and Grammar.

ZEN AND WOMEN

Perhaps the title should be rather "Women and Zen," but anyway the subject is a double one, Zen seen by women, and women seen by Zen. The latter seems easier to tackle, but perhaps this is an illusion. Is the title almost equal to "Zen and the Higher Animals"? or "Zen and Nature"? Is Zen unnecessary to women? Are they all born with it? How do women listen to music, read poetry, look at pictures? In these the timeless is seen in time, the spaceless in space, the formless in form,—without being separated from time, space, and form. Can women do this? Women do not, I think, feel time so deeply; its dreadful inevitability. To that extent they cannot grasp the timeless, the timelessness of time, its timefulness. When we listen to Brahms' *Alto Rhapsody,* with a *male* choir, do we hear what a woman knows of Brahms, or what Brahms knows of a woman?

What do women think of death? Do they think of it? Desdemona's death is not a tragedy. Lady Macbeth "should have died hereafter." Even Cleopatra's death, for all Shakespeare's poetry, does not make us weep. Euripides allows Medea to escape into the heavenly mansions. Oddly enough, Juliet, a girl of fourteen, is more tragic than Romeo and the rest of them. In ancient India Juliet's suttee was once the rule rather than the exception. It represents the nothingness of a woman without a man. When Lucy died, —"O the difference to *me!*"

A woman lives in the present far more than in the past or the future, and thus has little *mayoi,* perhaps too little to have *satori.* Women cannot sin. They cannot be saved. There are scarcely any women in the *Inferno.* Beatrice seems as if born in the *Paradiso.*

Angels are masculine, a kind of neuter male. I asked a woman rōshi if the *satori* of a man and a woman are the same. "Of course!" she replied indignantly, but how could she know, an old woman of eighty who had never touched a man? How did she know what a man's *satori* is? Can a man know what another man's is? It is all guessing at best, and the superstition of oneness at worst.

Women know little of women. Jane Austen only knows a man-like woman, herself. One might go so far as to say that a woman cannot know a woman by definition. Do men know anything about women? Certain men know certain types. Chaucer knew several types, the Wife of Bath and the Prioress and so on. Shakespeare knew many. Richardson is said to have understood the female heart, but for that reason perhaps, I could never bear to read him. George Eliot knew some kinds of women, Hardy and D. H. Lawrence some others. The fact is that women are like nature; we can't understand them because there is nothing to understand. Zen is the same; we can't explain it because there is nothing to explain. The intellectual elements are completely dissolved in Nature and women and Zen. Only in men are they precipitated. The Zen of men also is inexplicable because the intellect is subsumed into the intuition. The Zen of a woman is inexplicable because she has no intellect. The Zen of women is a sort of pre-Zen. The Virgin Mary ascended into heaven, but she was not crucified. She never really died. The Zen of a man thus corresponds to Western Zen, that of a woman to Eastern Zen. In some ways a man's Zen is better; it moves, and moves others. In some ways a woman's is better; it moves others without moving itself. A man must have a woman's Zen, and a woman must have a man's Zen. Impossible? All the better, for Zen is doing what is impossible, an imperfect human being doing something perfectly, and drinking up all the tea in the world out of one small cup. Women do not, like men, desire to do what is nonsensical, what is impossible, but all the more they do it. As an example of this we may take a short story, *A Bunch of Grapes,* by Arishima Takeo, who died in a suicide pact in 1923 with Aki Hatano. A Japanese boy stole some water-colours from a school-mate, a foreign boy. He was caught by the other boys, and brought before the teacher. Instead of grumbling at him she gave him a bunch of grapes, and told him to be sure to come to school the next day. He came, and, forgiven by the other boys, was given some more grapes by that "lovely white hand." What is the point of the story? The boy does something wrong; he steals. What does this woman do? She rewards him for stealing,—not to heap coals of fire on his head, not to make him realise his sinfulness, but just because a boy, any boy, is something we must give grapes to. She has no sin in herself; she does not see it in others. The idea of retribution, the idea of law, of cause and effect is absent from her mind. Not only so, but the notions of guilt and remorse and atonement are very faint. There is no Emersonian doctrine of the in-staneity of sin and its punishment by a feeling of transgression. "Have you thought what a bad thing it was that you did?" she asks. Then, "There, no more tears." This is all she says.

We must now ask, what is the proper attitude and the right thing to do for a man, that is, what is a man's Zen in such a case? Answering for myself, I would have said to the boy, and to the other boys all together, "Well, he looks pretty miserable, and so do you. To feel guilty, and to feel indignation at the guilt of another is not a very pleasant feeling. I suppose most of you boys have stolen things and had things stolen from you. When I was young I used to steal pennies out of my mother's purse to buy sweets, and spoil my teeth. I have stolen other things in later life. Once I stole a book on sex from a book-shop because I was ashamed to buy it openly. When we don't steal we feel free. After all, freedom is best,

freedom of feeling. That's all. Bye-bye!" Not all
the boys would understand this. One or two would
merely think, "The teacher is a thief too, so it's all
right for me to steal." Which of the two, the woman's Zen, and the man's Zen, is better? But by
what standard do we judge? If we try to decide by
the effect, we see at once that the result of our actions
is various, largely unforseen, and almost all un-
knowable. We can judge Zen only by Zen, and from
this point of view, that is, intuitively speaking, the
woman's Zen is better. But note "the lovely white
hand." This is not Zen at all, but sentimentality. Yet
the man's Zen is too talkative, too reasonable, even
though it rightly generalises the particular. The
woman's is too vague, but particularises (in the grapes)
the general. The answer then must be that both are
better. A rather small bunch of grapes, and just a
very few words of self-depreciation.

We may consider the question of women's Zen in
a more technical, a more esoteric way. The most common kōan given to would-be Buddhas is that of *Mu.*
What will a woman make of it? You may say, "The
same as a man, for *Mu* is sexless," but this is a mistake,
because a woman is not sexless, and a sexful person
cannot grasp a sexless thing, any more than a sexless
person can understand a sexful thing. A woman's
mathematics is feminine, and a man's is masculine. A
woman's man is female, a man's woman is male. This
truth is a combination of Spengler and D. H. Lawrence,
the idea that a person of one culture can never understand (the person of) another culture, and the idea
that each thing has not only its own life and joy, as
Wordsworth thought, but will and sex. But it may
be asked, "Is there no such thing as transcending
sex?" A man taught us to pray, "Our Father which
art in Heaven." "The Church is the Bride of Christ."
The angels in Heaven, who neither marry nor are given
in marriage,—one would like to see them! Is there
no such thing as humanity? There is not, any more

than an animal, or even *a* dog; there is only *this* dog.

Well, by answering in this intransient way, we
have let ourselves in for trouble. We have to explain
what a man's *Mu* is, and what a woman's *Mu* is.

A monk asked Chaochu, "Has this dog the Buddha-
nature, or not?" Chaochu answered, *"Mu* (No)!"*

Wumen, who was a man, not a woman, commented
that those who understand the meaning of *Mu* "walk
hand in hand with all the patriarchs of Zen, the hair
of their eyebrows tangled with one another, seeing
with the same eyes, hearing with the same ears. Isn't
that a joyful thing?" The answer is, "When you agree
with me I know I am wrong." Sameness must be also
difference, otherwise it is not the real sameness. Anyway, what is *Mu*? *Mu* means *ima*, now. All the energy
of mind and body is concentrated on this instant, just
as a lion uses all a lion's strength to scratch his ear.
When we think of past things, as Thoreau says, "All
the past is here present to be tried; let it approve itself
if it can!" As for the future, however near and disagreeable it may be, we are like the Zen priest who
was dying, and when they brought him pen and ink
to write his death-poem, waved them away, saying,
"I don't want to die!" *Mu* means *shi*, death, but this
death is wanting to live while you are alive, and
wanting to be dead when you are dead. If you are
willing to die, you have no right to live. *Mu* means
to die to all questions, and to all answers. It is the
life of wonder, but not of curiosity. Everything in the
universe says *Mu*, "I am not," which means *U*, "I am."
So God is the great "I am," because he is not
omniscient, not omnipotent, not good, and at the same
time not ignorant of anything, in no way impotent,
too pure even to behold evil.

All this is the verbosity of a man's Zen, the legs
of a male snake. What about a woman's legs? In the
Victorian age she was supposed to have none. Wumen
says that "we must block up and cut off our line of

thought." Women haven't much of a line to cut anyway. In his verse at the end Wumen says:

> The Buddha-nature of the dog:
> All is held in the command, "Wu !"
> A moment's lapse into Yes-or-no,—
> Mourn the body ! Your life is lost !

We may take this as meaning that if a woman gives
up her intuition and falls into intellectual dichotomy,
she ceases to be a woman, she ceases to be anything.
Women must avoid men like the plague, but men must
imitate women as far as possible. Of course a woman
may pretend to think. In fact it is required in society
and necessary in marriage, but it must be only pretending. A man must think, and believe that he is
thinking, and his thought will remain to trouble him
to the end of time. A woman is *Mu* itself; she is submerged in it, suffused with it; this is her great power,
her great attraction. She already is what man would
attain to with his intellect. It is not possible, and that
is why it must be done.

ZEN IN EUROPEAN ART

An eminent Japanese art critic and devotee of Zen once said to me that there could be no Zen in Western art or literature since the word itself did not exist in any European language. This opinion betrays both an exclusiveness and an excessive respect for words which Zen itself deprecates. A thing, for example a physical or mental disease, or art itself, may exist while there is as yet no word for it; and many words in the dictionary, for instance, "unnatural," "divine," "purity," have practically no objects corresponding to them. Further, the word Zen is not Japanese; it is borrowed from China. But Zen is not a Chinese word; it was imported from India. Where did the Indians get it from?

If "Zen" represents the whole value, or the vital poetry (in the deepest meaning of the word) the title of this essay would be without meaning. We would be saying, in the larger sense of the term, that Zen *is* European art, rather than what is, from a limited viewpoint, a discussion of what is best *in* European art. It will be better therefore to restrict the meaning of Zen for the time being to that state of mind-body referred to by the Zen Sect, in which no division exists between the actor and the scenery, in which one thing is acted as all things, and all things are manipulated in one thing.

According to Mr. Shinichi Hisamatsu's recent book, *Zen to Bijutsu,* "Zen and (Chinese and Japanese) Art," Zen has seven characteristics as seen in painting, pottery, calligraphy, Nō, the tea ceremony, and so on; they are:

1. Asymmetry (avoidance of the geometrical and perfect; unsaintly saints)

2. Simplicity (black and white preferred)

100

3. Agedness (finished before it is begun; Words-worth's "bare trees and mountains bare")

4. Naturalness (innocence; thought-less-ness; no compulsion)

5. Latency (the gentleness of the warrior; the sub-dued but not gloomy light of the tea-room; much in little)

6. Unconventionality (indifference to contradictions; no "Idea of the Holy")

7. Quietness (inner, not outer)

We should use these terms flexibly; they may include their apparent opposites. Quietness is heard in the roaring end of a Bach fugue, with *organo pleno*. It is seen in the writhing of a million maggots in rotting fish-heads. Unconventionality may be expressed in the wearing of a silk hat and frock coat. Zen has latency (*yūgen*) but is not symbolic. It is deep, but easy. Zen is natural, but there is little Zen in children and none in animals, which are near-machines. We must become children, but a man who has become a child is not merely a child.

Each of the above qualities is necessary; none can be omitted, because they are different names of the same nameless thing which is not a thing. When one is absent, all are absent. To these seven I wish to add four more, which will give us a nice Zen number, eleven.

8. Freedom (absolute freedom—to be symmetrical if we want to)

9. Humour (includes paradox and contradiction, and the blessedness which we attain to in their perception)

10. Sexuality ("Eternity is in love with the produc-tions of time"; this sexual relation between man and the world is Zen, and enlightenment is its orgasm; "All nature is my bride," says Thoreau.

Those human and necessary elements, sadism and
masochism, are included here.)

11. Joy (youthfulness, Blake's *Glad Day*; the early
Wordsworth's universe)

Zen is not an Oriental thing, but again Western Zen
is not Eastern Zen. A man's Zen is not a woman's Zen.
My Zen is not your Zen. It is the same, yes, but it is
different. We must be on our guard against oneness,
against the absolute. We must protect the individual.
We must protect ourselves. We shall find the last
four qualities far more in evidence in Western than in
Eastern Zen, but they should be present (if only as
No. 5, latency) in Eastern Zen also. These eleven
characteristics are not necessarily visible and tangible;
but they cannot be absent. Any work of art, therefore,
which is a-sexual, or anti-sexual, which is completely
without any cosmically comical elements, which is
joyless, or is limited, or stinks of Zen, lacks Zen.
Further, the judgement of a work of art is, however
often repeated or revised, an immediate, single, unified
act, a unifying of the perceiver and the thing perceived.
These seven or eleven or sixty-five qualities, or what
not, are thus only so many separate intellectual justifica-
tions and confirmations of a single artistic unity. In
this sense Zen is momentary, or rather momental, or
more strictly speaking, non-successive, not cumulative,
because timeless. (Da Vinci spent four years on *Mona
Lisa*, trying to get woman's Zen into it.)

Applying the last four qualities, prominent in Western
art, to some alleged examples of Zen in Eastern art,
we may say that Liang K'ai *Sakyamuni Coming Out
of the Mountains* looks at first sight quite sexless, but
when we examine his eye we see a subdued passion in
it like that in the eye of Bach. Again, where is the
humour? Look at his feet. On the other hand, the famous
Zen garden of Ryōanji Temple, consisting of sand and
huge stones only, seems to me too deathly, sexless, joyless; it is the universe as a machine. These stones are

not "deep in admiration." Again, Hiroshige's landscapes are not Zen because they are too good, too poetical; nothing is left to the imagination. The Ise Shrines, with all their purity, simplicity and quietness, lack freedom,—and lack one, lack all. Zen art is the primitivism and unselfconsciousness of the savage together with the timelessness and cosmic consciousness of the saint or sage. Zen is religious, not moral; poetical not beautiful; intuitionistic, not intellectual; significant, not emotional; sensual, not philosophical; youthful, not world-weary.

One last point. We say, "There is Zen in this picture, no Zen in that," but this is not really correct. If we, and the picture or words or whatever it is, are un-divided, there is Zen, and not otherwise. Or to speak more exactly, when I am it and it is I, and at the same time I am I and it is it, there is Zen. Thus, "There is no Zen in this picture" is really the judgement that it was painted for and with money or fame or imitation or habit or stupidity, not with Zen, and it is therefore difficult to get Zen into or out of it. Also, to say, "This has some Zen," or "more Zen" is absurd because Zen is not a thing, not a principle, not a force, not a cause or an effect of anything. What we really mean then by saying, "There is Zen in Rembrandt's self-portrait (that of 1658), in Hogarth's *Shrimp-girl*," is that Zen is easily seen in that face, that eye. It sinks into the mind effortlessly, the mind that "watches and receives."

Coming now to the subject proper, Zen in Western Art, we may take a few examples of Zen in European painting, omitting sculpture, pottery, architecture and so on almost entirely. Picasso's *Head of a Faun* on a plate in being modern is subject to the suspicion that it has received some indirect influence from Zen, but anyway it has all the eleven elements of Zen without being in the least imitative of Oriental art, or tending to abstraction; it has always given me an extreme joy. The same objection, that he may have been affected by Chinese and Japanese painting, can be made to Klee,

who is full of Zen, so let us take Rousseau, who is so
realistic and minute, his materials so individual and
even provincial, that his Zen is different from anything
we find in the Zen paintings of China and Japan.
The jungle pictures are all excellent, especially the
Charmeuse de Serpents and *Eve,* both of 1907, the feeling of age being given in the former by the wooden
face and rope-like hair of the naked woman; in the
latter by the old-world flamingoes and the snakes, and
the dark color of the right half of the picture. But it
is in *La Bohémienne Endormie,* 1897, that we see
Rousseau's Zen most vividly. This will be quite clear
if we simply repeat the list of eleven points; asymmetry,
simplicity, agedness, naturalness, latency, unconventionality, quietness, freedom, humour, sex, joy. This
picture has the only good kind of mysticism, that which
does not stink of religion. The Zen is in the lion's tail,
which stretches out in the Void (*kū*), just like Gutei's
finger (*Mumonkan,* No. 3). The eye of the lion is that
of Mu Ch'i's *Bull-headed Shrike on a Pine Tree.* The
eye sees through us into the universe. *"Tiere sehen dich
an."*

For the Zen artist, the problem is how to make
manifest the meaning of the empty space in a picture.
Mousehold Heath by Crome in the National Gallery is
a fine sky which too often in European landscape
painting is filled with trees, or at least with clouds.
The earth exists to give meaning to the sky, which
again has no significance without the withered stretch
of ancient heath, the path over it, the shepherd and
the animals. The small sketch by Girtin reproduced
in *Zen in English Literature* has a Zen-less Zen that
leaves us with nothing to say about it.

To see this same Zen in Goya's *Los Proverbios* and
Los Desastres de la Guerra needs some courage, some
energy of mind. The Chinese and Japanese are too
sentimental (in art) to have anything like the truth
of these sketches. Oriental artists have to the full the
willing acceptance of Marcus Aurelius and Epictetus,

but not enough of the Greek loathing of death, not
sufficient appreciation of pure violence, of motiveless
malignity. The ancient Central Americans and the
Spaniards excelled in this latter. Zuoaga, a modern
painter, who died in 1945, never made a sketch for any
of his pictures. *The Dwarf* is full of Zen. We see the
Divine Ugliness, the Cosmic Bestiality in this hideous,
under-sized creature carrying two over-sized dead
hogs. But he is not rejected by us. Under him also
are the Everlasting Arms. And has not a pig, dead or
alive, the Buddha-Nature? El Greco has this Spanish
Zen. His *View of Toledo* is really a View of the
Universe. Bridges leap, roads wind, houses rise,
churches soar, above them a wild and whirling sky.
In all this we invisible human beings are irresistibly
and inveterately involved. There is no union of man
and nature, for there was never any division. The still
small voice and the thunders of this Sinai are the
deafening silence of Vimalakirti.

The Zen of Blake's paintings seems at first sight
somewhat eccentric, but upon closer and deeper
examination we see they have also the general Zen
characteristics. God is white-haired, but has no
wrinkles. Satan is as handsome as the best of them.
All of Blake's figures have both poise and energy. They
fly without wings. Joy is felt in every line. Everything is strange and new, but nothing is distorted. The
trees and flowers, the sun and moon are as sexual as
the human beings, who also are naked and unashamed.
Nothing is fixed or dead, "for unto him all live."

A Zen picture that would make an orthodox Zen
artist turn in his grave is one by Pahari, an 18-19th
century Indian artist. It shows us the warrior Mahadeva,
crescent-crowned, snake on arm, with Parvarti sleeping
peacefully on his knee. He gazes down at her with
the purest joy, shown also in that outstretched arm.
Far in the distance we see the night sky over a pond
of lotuses. A white bull stands there with passionate
dignity. Birds sleep in the trees, leopards roam the

woods. Age cannot wither the lovers. The Zen of this
picture is to be compared and contrasted with that of
Goya and Zuoaga, where we see the everlasting youth
of wickedness and brutality.

Returning to the 18th century English landscape
school, Constable's *View at Epsom,* in the Tate Gallery,
should be compared with Mu Ch'i's *Persimmons*; both
are sexual, the first female, the second male, but the
stallion to the left of Constable's picture is essential
to it. Alexander Cozens' sketches for his landscapes
are full of Zen, just as the brush is full of swiftly-
moving paint, which dries immediately. The one shown
here, c. 1750, is of a rocky promontory. Hobbema's
well-known *L'Allée de Middenharnis* has Zen in it.
When we look at this avenue of not so beautiful, indeed
scraggy trees, we are reminded of Wordsworth's Zen
experience with an unknown woman, recorded in
Stepping Westward. There it was the sound of her
voice that humanized the thought:

> Of travelling through the world that lay
> Before me in my endless way.

Claude Lorrain, born in 1600, was apparently an
uneducated and ignorant man, who got others to draw
the human figures in his landscapes, but the *Liber
Veritatis,* which Turner tried so vainly to surpass in
Liber Studiorum, has drawings of trees and hills (pen
and wash) in which we feel all nature involved. His
regular paintings are overlaid with romance and
mythology, but these sketches show his earthy feeling
for earth, fiery for fire, airy for air, watery for water.
Indeed it is in the sketches by Girtin, Crome, Rembrandt,
Ruysdael and others that we often find Zen, smothered
by externals and details in completed pictures.

Let us take a picture in the Louvre, No. 1322, by
Ghirlandajo, *An Old Man and His Grandchild.* The
realism of the old man contrasts with the formality
of the landscape, and with the poor painting of the
child's hand. The Zen is in the nose of the old man,

or rather, in the eye of his grandchild, who gazes at
it with the greatest simplicity. He really sees it, and,
"All that we behold is full of blessings." The ugly
excrescences on the nose, beloved by the child, "spoils
the picture," according to an English art critic. "Listen
to the fool's reproach, it is a kingly title!" Zen is indeed
what spoils. It spoils beauty, it spoils morality, intellectuality, emotionality, abstract truth, religion, art,
literature, science.

Going farther back, Piero della Francesca's *Nativity*,
in the National Gallery has the serene inner power of
symbolic Christianity. God lies on the cushion in the
form of a babe. Statuesque but graceful maidens sing
a solemn but joyous song. The ground is dry and sandy,
the stable ruined, grass grows on the roof, but,

> All's right with his heaven !
> God's on the earth.

We feel Zen in the benignant severity of Giotto, the
greatest concentration of it being in the kiss of Judas
in the garden of Gethsemane, (the fresco in the church
of Maria del Arena). Christ and Judas gaze at each
other with the same intentness and intensity with which
the monk looks on as the two cocks fight in the pictures
by Liang K'ai and Niten (Miyamoto Musashi).

One of the elements of Zen in Christianity is the
God-man nature of Christ. With the Flemish school
Christ becomes indeed too human. Blake says:

> Thou art a Man, God is no more,
> Learn thy own Humanity to adore.

This is Zen; adoration also is necessary. Some of the
best examples of Zen in Christian art, especially that
greatest of all subjects, the Crucifixion, are found in
Byzantine Churches from the 6th to the 11th century.
At this time Roman naturalism was being blended with
Near Eastern methodology; the material and the spiritual
attained a temporary balance. When we look (as we
should, if possible) at such mosaics with a Japanese

eye, we find many things both repulsive and apparently
un-Zen-like. In the first place, a man hanging on a
cross; quite apart from the first seven characteristics of
Zen, has this the alleged last four, freedom, humour, sex,
and joy? But it is God who hangs there—what A Joke
indeed! He is naked, but the sexual parts are hidden,
are latent. It is "for the joy set before him" that he
endures the cross and despises the non-existent shame.
He is, of course, perfectly free not to do the will of his
Father in Heaven. But how about the blood from the
nails and the wound in the side, the blood that flows
perpetually? As Marlowe says in *Faustus*:

> See, see where Christ's blood streams in the
> firmament!
> One drop would save my soul, half a drop, ah,
> my Christ!

This is the agony, the Hell of the unenlightened
man; Zen is the blood of the universe. Note also that
it is a real man, but the figure does not sag from the
nails. It floats there. "Hail to thee, blithe Spirit! Man
thou never wert." The expression is one of deep but
calm grief. Christ was nailed to a tree, and as D. H.
Lawrence said, "I know why Jesus was crucified on
a tree"; man is put to death upon nature. (But we,
in this our age, are reserved for a more cruel and
dreadful death, on a cross of ferro-concrete.) When
we compare this Crucifixion from the Greek church at
Daphni, in Attica, 11th century A.D. with Liang K'ai's
Sakyamuni Coming Out of the Mountains, 13th century,
we see a marked difference in the first element, asymmetry, though the skull and flowering weeds at the foot
of the cross add a grotesque and discordant note to the
whole. The (orthodox) Christian, the Buddhist, the
scientific will is towards symmetry, but the Zen will
is towards asymmetry. Again, in the picture of Christ
there is little of that innocence (naturalness) which He
himself recommended. Liang K'ai's Buddha, however,
has this mildness and humility, even to the point of
weakness and gloom.

Eastern Zen art always portrays *satori*, enlightenment, either in the person depicted or in the object as seen by the eye of the enlightened man. Western Zen art, on the contrary, very often shows us *mayoi*, illusion, irresoluteness, the divided mind, the unsatisfiable desire, that of *Faustus* and *Hamlet*. Such is the Greek statue (bronze) of the Boxer Resting, 3rd Century B.C. The strength and weariness, the hairy brutality and the pitiless pity (of the sculptor), the broken nose and thongs round the hand and arm, the powerful body and frown of stupidity,—it is the universe itself, and concentrated in the very turn of the head. Should this, and other examples of *mayoi*, seem strange to Japanese "Zenists", let them remember the most difficult doctrine of Zen, that illusion *is* enlightenment, enlightenment *is* illusion.

We must not confuse Zen or *Zen-mi*, the taste of Zen, with Zen taste, *Zen-teki na shumi*. There is a tendency for people to like quietness and solitude as they grow older. But age is not in itself good, any more than youth is. It is the perfect combination of both which gives us the excellence of *Don Quixote* and the Parthenon. The East is more passive, the West more active. But passivity, as Wordsworth said, must be "wise", and activity that of "unmoved mover."

There remain many problems still unsolved: Is there any relation between Zen and the creation or appreciation of art? Does one increase the other? Can a man go to (be in) Heaven who has bad taste? Is Zen itself good taste? Is Zen perhaps God's Taste?

ZEN AND MUSIC

Primitive music was heard as something magical, and this is already Zen, for Zen is magic, what Emerson called "charm," that makes the sun forgotten. And from the beginning, we must suppose, both in the rhythm of the dancing and the rise and fall of the sounds, the magic was the sound-silence, the motionless movement, the difference sameness. There is no other magic. All the rest is bunkum. We do not know anything of ancient Greek or Chinese music, but when we think of Plato's ban on tragedy, and of what Confucious and the Tang poets said of music, we can guess now much we have lost,—in Zen rather than music in the ordinary sense of the word. Greek music was all melodic, with a similar value perhaps to that of a Bach solo violin or cello. Chinese music, like Korean, was harmonic in a philosophic sense, the clay, metal, wood, and instruments of other materials giving us literally the music of the spheres.

The most remarkable thing about real music, by which I mean polyphonic Zen, is the change from melody to harmony, that is, from horizontal to vertical. It is said that two-part singing was practised in the 9th century in Europe. In England part-singing was already popular in the 12th century. To say two things at once is not possible in words, but it can be done both in painting and in musical polyphony. It is interesting to note the Spenglerian fact that when three-part organa and three-part motets were being written in the 13th century, there was also a combining of the religious and secular, a mixing of the hymns of the church and the songs of the jongleurs. When sacred really equals profane, we have Zen.

In the 14th, 15th, and 16th centuries there was a

gradual increase in the number of parts, and of their independence from the cantus firmus. There was also a fusion of complexity and simplicity, head and heart, counterpoint and poetry. When the (intellectual) sense equals the (physical) sound there is Zen. In Willaert, 1480-1562, we have what may be called *shibui* music. It is not Zen, for it lacks energy. It its not going anywhere. The music of Palestrian also, 1525-94, has an excessive purity and other-worldliness. It lacks earthiness, and joie-de-vivre. (It is odd, by the way, how many qualities are necessary for Zen. And if one is missing all are missing.) In England, the madrigals of Morley, Wilbye, and Weelkes have a Shakespearean naturalness and at the same time ingenuity, but they lack the German mysticism of Scheidt which led to the Zen of Bach. Byrd and Purcell have not only mysticism, but Zen also, especially in some of their lighter, purely instrumental works. The chorale is of the essence of Zen, but the soprano is perhaps too strong. Zen in music can be tested to some extent by the importance of the bass. The basso ostinato of the 17th century, the passacaglias of Buxtehude and Bach are particular important in this respect. It is a pleasure to play the accompaniment only, even the left hand only, of Bach's viola da gamba sonatas; this "pleasure" is Zen. Handel's bass is strong, but often merely pom-pom-pom.

The opera, which more or less begins with Monteverdi's *Orfeo,* 1607, has not a spark of Zen in it, even when Mozart writes it. The operatic element in *The Messiah* makes it odious, and even spoils the *Matthew Passion.* Music is not emotion. Music is Zen. A certain amount of emotion and thought and beauty may be added to music, as we put salt in cakes to bring out the sweetness, but salt and sugar are different things. The sonatas and trio sonatas of Veracini, Tartini, and so on are mechanical elaborations of a type. Corelli is feminine and sweet, Vivaldi masculine but empty. Even Handel's sonatas for violin or flute or both leave us

cold. Schutz is deeper, Pachelbel is somehow interesting, but Buxtehude is the only musician who approaches
Bach.

Bach is Zen itself. Like Zen he absorbed everything.
Like Zen, everything he wrote wrote itself. The only
way to describe this naturalness, the selfful selflessness
of Bach's music is to quote from *A Week on the Concord*
concerning literature:

> As naturally as the oak bears an acorn and the
> vine a gourd, man bears a poem, either spoken or
> done.... Homer's song is a vital function like breath-
> ing, and an integral result like weight.... He is as
> serene as nature, and we can hardly detect the
> enthusiasm of the bard.

Bach is more full of contradictions than Hamlet. Classic
and romantic, abstract and pictorial, traditional and
original, ancient and modern, introspective and impersonal, calm and poignant, he is like Shakespeare in
that every work is a self-portrait, yet he remains an
enigma; others abide our question.

The Zen of Bach, however, does not lie in these
paradoxes or in the mystery of his character. It consists in the fact that everything he wrote is faultless.
He has the ear that never sleeps, the hand that never
slackens; he is never weary in well-doing. His Zen is
adumbrated in Cecil Gray's rhetorical question in *The
History of Music*:

> Was he a musical alchemist who had discovered a
> kind of philosopher's stone, some formula of con-
> struction which enabled him to transmute the basest
> material into purest gold?

To give specific examples, Zen is found everywhere
in the Brandenburg Concertos, except the (popular)
5th for flute and violin. We may particularly point out
the adagio of the 1st. It is at once cosmic and intense.
The trio, for two horns and three oboes in unison, is
a good instance of Zen in its using any material for
any purpose, light nimbleness in the horn, stolid insensitiveness in the oboes. But after all, the trumpet

is the best (the most Zennish) of all instruments, not
the mere shouting of Handel, but the trumpets of Bach
in the 2nd Brandenburg concert and elsewhere. The
andante is most touching, but becomes a little sloppy
without the starch of the trumpet. The 3rd like the
first and third movements of the 6th, is a ballet, all
the dancers wearing the same sombre dress, but joy
animates their limbs. The andante of the 4th is noteworthy in the way is avoids the latent sentimentality
of the flutes. *The Art of Fugue* is pure Zen from beginning to end. When we hear it first it seems dark and
gloomy, dry and lifeless, but if we play it often, at
last it loses this character, and we hear it as we see
the rising and setting of the sun, the procession of
the seasons, life and death, men coming and going on
the earth. *The Art of Fugue* means free necessity, a
willed necessity.

Any man who thinks Handel "stands as little below
Bach as Bach is below him," has no understanding of
Bach, in other words, knows nothing of Zen, that is,
of music. Handel has no Zen. He has the solidity
which Telemann lacked, due to his respect for the
bass, but he has no poetry, no depth, no complexity;
he is only, musically speaking, "a jolly good fellow."
For the same reason, Haydn has no Zen. Mozart is
full of it, and yet sometimes, when we come in at the
middle of a quartet or early symphony, we can hardly
tell at first whose it is. As far as the form goes, Haydn,
Mozart, and Beethoven adopt the new kind of solo
melody in their sonatas, with alternations of it between
the instrument and the piano. The world was growing
cheaper, more vulgar, sensational, sentimental, romantic.
People were tired of listening to contrapuntal music;
they were tired of Zen. They wanted their ears tickled,
their heart-strings pulled, their lachrymal glands
squeezed. An example is Haydn's Emperor's Hymn
used in a set of variations for a string quartet. Another
example is the Fugues of Wilhelm Friedrich, Bach's
eldest and most gifted son. They have all the senti-

mentality which Bach had not, and lack all the poetry
which Bach had. The Zen of Mozart by which he
defied the times, and which caused his death, is not
in the violin concertos, or even the piano concertos,
but in the trio for piano, clarinet, and viola, the quintets
for strings, the oboe quartet, where inexorable fate
moves slowly or swiftly, but never unwillingly. We
feel that Mozart died before he composed each piece
of music. Beethoven's Zen is almost always smothered
by his emotion, by his strong will, by the crudeness of
his thinking. Beethoven alternates between war and
peace, the male and the female, joy and grief, but
sometimes his anger is just, and his sweetness is
piercing.

The romantics fell lower still, though not so low as
we. Schubert never wrote a line of music. It is all
feeling, either bombast or self-pity. His songs are truly
wild roses and garden roses, but a rose has no Zen.
Schumann, who admired Schubert so much, has moments, in some of his symphonies, when a valiant spirit
raises him above emotion into a heroic world that is
selfless. Selflessness is Zen. Mendelssohn has no
asceticism, but also has a few moments, as in the
Hebrides Overture and in the beginning of the *Scotch
Symphony*. The *Midsummer Night's Dream* music is
only the chattering of monkeys. It has little of the
pseudo-poetry of Shakespeare, and none of his real
magic, the fairy world of living creatures. Weber is
cheap, with the breathless mysticism of the German
forests, and a gorgeousness that wearies in the end.
Zen is always homely and friendly, in spite of its stern-
ness. Bizet has some Zen in him. Carmen is in the line
of Medea and Lady Macbeth. It is a woman's Zen,
beyond passion. The "I am I" is so strongly expressed
that we find it the counterpart of the Upanishad "I
am you." It is not Zen, but it is Half-Zen. Most so-
called Zen is this Half-Zen.

Liszt is nothing but wallowing in emotion, like
Rachmaninoff, but Berlioz has something in him. He

follows himself, and owns no other kin. He has the
fault of exhibitionism, but his programme music is
often music when the pure music of others is classical
dullness. Wagner is all that Zen is not. A false
simplicity, a bulging, over-sexual grandeur, a unity
gained by combining all the values except Zen,
masochism and sadism, the devotedness of woman, the
sinfulness of man, eternity and infinity, false tragedy,
fantastic mythology, cabbalism, Catholicism, Buddhism,
—what a pot-pourri it all is! And "pourri" is the right
word, for what he who is not for us is against us, and
what is not Zen has a pernicious, a poisoning effect
upon the world. Spiritually long-haired men like
Chopin are the women of music, as Handel is the
man (Beethoven was a hermaphrodite). It is said that
he never read a book; do women ever really read a
book? However, Chopin is not a poseur, like Wagner,
or Hugo. His moods and fancies and raptures and
despairs are all portrayed as they were, as they should
not have been. He is sincerely and unshamedly Zenless;
there is a little Zen here, women's Zen.

ZEN AND JAPAN

Zen originated in India and developed in China, together with the Taoism of Laotse and Chuangtse. It came to Japan as a sort of third-hand thing, something which the Japanese themselves did not create, and yet it is Zen in Japan that is Zen at its best, at its most living, most human, above all, most poetical.

In Upanishad times, from about 1,000 B.C., the sages meditating in the deep forests of India realized the only too easily-stated fact that we are ourselves the things (that seem to be) around us. This is the foundation of all religion (union with God), of art (become a bamboo and paint yourself), of music (the whole personality rising and falling, pausing and rushing onwards), and of poetry (the poet almost swallowed up in nature or other human beings). In India, however, art, music, and literature were not suffused with this spirit to the same degree or in the same way as in China, where the religious experience found its expression also through the brush, in pictures and poems.

As for music in China, the older forms soon passed away. Even in the Tang Era the poet Po Chüi regretted that people of his times did not appreciate that older music. One of the most astounding things in Chinese history is the saying of Confucius more than 1,000 years before this:

> When the Master was in Ch'i, he heard the Shao, and for three months did not know the taste of flesh. 'I did not think,' he said, 'that music could have been made so excellent as this.'

In the old Korean music, however, there is preserved something of the profound philosophic meaning of the sounds of the instruments, bamboo, stone, clay, and so on, by which the universe of matter expressed to the listening ear its *physical* meaning, each element in isolation, and their wild harmonies.

Zen, which is "unpremeditated art," when it came to, or reproduced itself, in China, lost all its misty and mystical Indian vagueness, and much of its escapism. It became as "heartless" as the Chinese, as the universe; it became sensuous, take-off-able and washable. Zen was now a comfortable old pair of shoes, the breaking of a rotten tooth, the smell of urine, a donkey's bray. Yet it was still a thing of monks and monasteries, something esoteric, communicated or at least stimulated from one enlightened monk to an as yet unenlightened one, and utterly incomprehensible to the uninitiated. However, the 6th Patriarch, Enō, had already said something less miserly, deeper and broader:

A thought of folly,—and one is an ordinary man; a thought of enlightenment,—and one is a Buddha.

Zen, after all, is simply the humanity of human beings, and cannot be restricted to monks and nuns, who are in many ways super-human, or rather sub-human, father-less, mother-less, wife-less, child-less creatures who tell us to be attached to nothing, like the fox that lost his tail in a trap.

When Zen came to Japan (officially in the 12th century, but Buddhist sects also had of course Zen elements already in them), it continued at first to be a matter of monks and monasteries, of *zazen* and *kōans*, but the Japanese people were different from the Chinese, and also from the Indians, though there were common elements.

The chief common element was a lack of rationality, and a corresponding lack of belief in its validity as a means of understanding a universe which is rational only in its rational and scientific aspect. Reason and logic, the Socratic method, were seen as correct, but as shallow, explaining nothing, only establishing a causal nexus which is totally unmeaning. Also com-

mon was the (dangerous and erroneous) idea or
(falsely interpreted) experience that Truth, though not
a thing in itself, is something once and for all attainable.
As Malvolio said, "Some are born great, some achieve
greatness, and some have greatness thrust upon 'em."
Zen is greatness.

The difference between the Chinese and the Indians
was chiefly in a certain softness of the Japanese
character. The Indians are soft, but somewhat sentimentally so, with their non-violence and ahimsa and
excessively voluptuous or ascetic tastes. The Chinese
are ruthless; without this violence of mind Zen would
have been impossible. Sadism and Zen are deeply
related, as we see also in Spain, for examle in *Don
Quixote*. The Japanese, however, (and this is a ticklish
point) have no sense as the British have of a black
and white justice, or abstract goodness. They can kill
in a frenzy of fear, or (what is nearly the same) in
a frenzy of patriotism, but mere killing, more destruc-
tion, roughness, rudeness,—there are the antithesis of
the Japanese spirit. Yet shininess, symmetry, slick-
ness, Greek perfection, Chinese richness, are equally
abhorrent. What the Japanese added to Zen was the
most difficult thing in the world, simplicity; this was
their own innate, potential Zen. Thoreau says that it
(homeliness) "is almost as great a merit in a book as
a house, if the reader would abide there." Japanese
simplicity is seen most clearly in Shintō, which is a
religion without a religious idea in it.

Zen is supposed to be the essence of Buddhism. But
actually Zen is closest, not to the moralizing of Confucius or the philosophising of Buddha but to the silent
bowing of the head before what is neither good nor
bad, neither true nor untrue. To put the matter in
another way, what happened to Zen when it came to
Japan was that on the one hand it became aristocratic,
in the artistic sense; Zen served poets and painters and
sculptors in confirming their tastes, and deepest judgements of value. On the other hand, Zen spread among

the common people, those who could not read or write, who were completely ignorant of the Mahayana philosophy, who did not and could not know, intellectually speaking, what Zen was, and had not heard even the word.

A native poetry and humor, these are what the Japanese added to Zen. The Chinese also had both, but their humour was too bucolic, too hard; their poetry was too Wordsworthian, too much concerned with mountains and skies, or with the vast sadness of

> Old, unhappy, far-off things
> And battles long ago.

The Japanese wanted to make every detail of daily life significant, not so much beautiful as a perpetual blessing, so that flowers shall be arranged in the lavatory, and wither in the ammonia; a brush and a bowl should be a delicate pleasure to the fingers. Straight lines and the texture of the posts, the roughness of the walls, the silences between the tinkling of the wind bells, even in a poor man's house, are the pleasures of life.

But after all, even this requires a certain amount of wealth and leisure to enjoy it. Strictly speaking, Zen belongs to poverty, both material and spiritual. In Japan the hermits of China have always been admired more than in their native land,—yet one more example of the truth of Christ's words.

From this point of view we may hesitate in our appreciation of famous Japanese gardens, or Nō, or The Tea Ceremony, or even Flower Arrangement. A rabid objection to wealth of any kind, and to the culture connected with it, is not altogether commendable, but like Christ, Zen (especially in Japan) always leans towards the small and lowly. Like Lamb, it loves "the obscure and remote, that which rests on its own intrinsic and silent merit." Zen is seen at its best in those "Little unremembered acts of kindness and of love," not only towards other people and to animals, but even more towards inanimate things, a stick or stone "which the best of us excel." These are perhaps the most important of our "human relations." So Wordsworth and his sister Dorothy found their highest bliss in gazing together at a glow-worm "laid safely by itself beneath a tree." This is Zen.

But what shall we do in this modern world of vulgarity, expansion, progress, mechanisation, uglification, a rising standard of dying? I would like to add to Wordsworth and Dorothy and the glow-worm the story of the little bird who saw a forest fire, and in her compassion she wished to extinguish it to prevent so much loss of life and beauty. She flew to a far-off lake and brought water in her beak drop by drop, to extinguish it. But she fell dead of exhaustion in a few days. This is the work of Zen. The Japanese have given up their dreams of glory spiritual (Bushidō), and glory material (Imperialism). Will they not bring a few drops of water to the universal conflagration?

ZEN AND NŌ

In his new edition of *Zen and Japanese Culture,* Dr. Suzuki says that "instead of expressing themselves by free inquiry and healthy reflection on life itself the Japanese rather sought to escape from the feudalistic oppression by such devices as the Nō dance, the art of tea, literature, and other social and artistic entertainments." This explanation may be correct psychologically, but it is not adequate poetico-dynamically. Any kind of life whatever may rightly be called an escape; the question is whether we escape from reality to unreality, or from unreality to reality. The tea ceremony, landscape gardening, Nō, the composition of 31-syllable verse were 14th century examples of the latter type of escape. The feudalistic system, the Communist, the Christian, the Buddhist systems are all forms of unreality (as systems) from which we must flee into the real, the poetical world, that is, the world of everyday poetical life of our own creation.

Nō was time seen as eternal, history glorified yet saddened by the Buddhist thought of impermanence, "battles long ago" remembered in the pitying heart. Nō combined three forms of culture, music, dancing, and poety, but by the genius of two men, father and son, Kan-ami and Zeami, it was lifted out of the triviality of opera. The "dancing" enabled the spectators to see the past as present, the distant as near, the impersonal as personal, the existent as nonexistent. The Nō-actor walks as though not walking; the mask smiles and weeps without the slightest change of expression. This is God-like; this is Zen.

In speaking about Zen, especially in its relation to forms of culture, it is necessary always to bear in mind the difference between Zen as a "system" of paradoxes

evolved in India and China during a period of three
thousand years, and Zen as Zen, that is, the spontaneous,
individually created timeless-activity-in-time of an
undivided mind-body. This is the substratum, the
continuum, the *basso ostinato* of the former, the historically developed consciousness of Zen.

Zen is not a religion; it is religion. Zen is not a
value; it is value. Beauty is a value, goodness is a
value, truth is a value; they often overlap, but seldom
coincide, in spite of Keats' assertion. What is often
mistaken for Zen is some value. A bull-fighter's Zen
is wisdom, but it has no love in it. Christ's Zen is
love, but it lacks wisdom. Buddhas' Zen is truth, but
where is the humanity? We may say, if we like, that
Zen is of two kinds, partial and total. The Zen of art,
the Zen of Nō is partial, just as the Zen of Hitler was
partial, and the Zen of a Zen abbot is partial. Total
Zen, that penetrates and interpenetrates the whole of
a man's life, and touches his purse, and changes his
clothes, that stops him reading the newspapers, and
writing articles for magazines,—this is not our concern
here.

The actual historical connection between Zen and Nō
is extremely difficult to make out, and not so charming
when we do so. Kan-ami and Zeami were patronised
by the 3rd Ashikaga Shōgun, Yoshimitsu, and it is
asserted and repeated that Yoshimitsu's interest in and
knowledge of Zen were somehow or other communicated to them. It is doubtful whether the understanding of Zen on the part of Kan-ami and Zeami,
both theoretical and practical, was very much wider
and deeper than that which Shakespeare displayed in
King Lear of the ancient Druidic religion. Moreover,
Yoshimitsu seems to have been a pretty awful sort of
chap, and his interest in Zen may well have been
because of its non-moral character, justifying the anti-
social arts of sculpture, the tea-ceremony, Nō, and so
on, and the family and national slaughter by which a
shōgun attained or retained his power. Further, even

the monks themselves, from Musō Kokushi onwards, are suspect. Their readiness to give political and military not to say homicidal advice to the Ashikaga Napoleons shows their Zen to have been opportunist in flavour. Adepts of Zen all have a certain Vicar of Bray attitude, an indifference to injustice, inequality, poverty, and suffering, which may be termed sublime. It was against such Zen priests that Ikkyū was to inveigh a hundred years later. (Ikkyū was once supposed to have written two Nō plays himself, *Yamauba,* and *Eguchi.*) However, such a conveniently transcendental standpoint was not peculiar to the Zen sect, and we must consider the relation of Nō to Buddhism in general.

The Buddhism of the Nō plays is of several kinds. There is the mystical, or rather symbolic and shamanistic Buddhism of the Shingon sect, seen in the priests in *Sotoba Komachi,* and the *yamabushi* of *Tanikō* and other plays. Then there is the ordinary popular Buddhism of the Amida sects, whose aim was salvation and the Western Paradise. The dramatic value of *karma,* rewards and punishments in the next life (lives) was fully and rightly utilised in a great many of the Nō plays. (Rightly, because every heroic or villainous life is felt as extending beyond the limit of physical death.) The paradoxical views of the Zen sect seem to be taken as detrimental to the holders of them (with the possible exception of Komachi in *Sotoba Komachi*), as for example Shunkan in the play of that name, and Nobutoshi in *Hokazō.* It is odd, by the way, that Komachi, whose Zen is so brilliant and poetical, is a woman. She belongs to a remarkable group. Medea, Cleopatra, the Wife of Bath, Lucy (Wordsworth's), and Mrs. Gamp. We cannot help feeling, however, that there is something dangerous about her Zen also—she is in fact a kind of murderess of her lover—and her arguments are amoral and destructive. She is therefore victorious as women always are and as Zen always is.

Nō plays themselves have something either lacking
or excessive in their nature, too much seriousness, or
too little humour for example, too much heroism or
too little humanity. (You can't have too much Zen.
You can't relieve the strain of Zen by reading a detec-
tive story. The only alternative to Zen is nothingness,
sleep or death.) If a Nō play cannot stand by itself,
it must be called lacking in Zen, that is, in some kind
of perfection, totality.

The Zen of kyōgen is that of the Artful Dodger in
Oliver Twist, of Master Bailey in *Martin Chuzzlewit,*
of Mr. Pepys; a certain shamelessness as opposed to
the excessive contrition of Nō. According to Nō, the
universe is a tragedy, in which certain values are
thereby made possible. For kyōgen the world is a
comedy, and this comicality, when perceived-created,
is itself a value. Kyōgen criticises power and rank,
though usually everything comes out all right for the
Lord in the end, as it does in the actual world. It
criticises Buddhism as being superstitious, and the
monks for the flagrant contradictions between their
precepts and their practice. Above all it is critical of
Nō for supposing that because some people are virtuous
there shall be no cakes and ale; in other words, it
objects to the religious idea that happiness is incompatible with blessedness. Zen never weeps, it always
laughs, laughs at the wonder of the world, its fantastic
nature. Thus Zen is in a way closer to kyōgen than
to Nō, but kyōgen lacks the depth of Nō. It was therefore an act of genius on the part of the founders of Nō
to alternate it with kyōgen. Zen is indeed not alternation; but in the world of time alternation is inevitable.
In the absolute world there is no alternation, but Zen
is not in the absolute world. It belongs to the absolute
relative world, so that a performance of five Nō plays
with three kyōgen between them is the nearest that
art can get to Zen,—as far as the question of tragedy
and comedy is concerned. It should be noted further
that women, who are so conspicuously omitted in Zen,

that is, the Zen of the Zen sect, play an important part, play their important part in both Nō and kyōgen. Nō is as far from being sexless as Zen should be; we see this in *Sotoba Komachi*, which is both a love-story and a Zen debate.

The Zen of Nō is the movement of the body-mind of the actor, especially visible in the (apparent) slow-motion, where eternity shows itself in love with the productions of time. On the Nō stage the illimitable is freely and perfectly limited. How is this done? As said before, in the mind-body of the performer, who travels from one province to another in a single step; who lives in the past more fully than we do in the present, who is more Hecuba than he is himself. "The mind is its own place." As literature also, Nō plays are full of Zen, not only in the poetry, and the inevitability of the outworking of the simple plot, but even in the word-play common throughout these dramas. As Herbert said, "by mere playing we go to Heaven." Christ is said to have founded his Church with a pun, and word-play is justified by the Zen notion that any word (thing) may mean anything because all words (things) are equal just as all men are, being infinite in (poetical) meaning.

The gorgeous costumes, the ceremonious diction, the aristocratic, unworldly atmosphere,—what have these to do with the simplicity, austerity, democracy, and everyday-ness of Zen? The costumes are a concession to human weakness and insensitivity. When we see a man in his underwear, or naked, we have the illusion that he is a poor forked radish, fantastically carved about the head. When we see a king in his robes, we perceive the richness, the dignity of every man; the purple without reminds us of the royalty within. In Zen itself we often get examples of the florid and flowery expressing the state of enlightenment. On the other hand, the extreme simplicity of gesture and dancing is the same thing in reverse. It is but one step from heaven to hell, and each step of a Nō actor is such a step.

Zen is also seen, and seen at its best, in the complete absence of the attempt to be original. Even the texts are a fluid hotch-potch of all kinds of "popular" songs, Buddhist sayings, historical and literary allusions, Chinese poetry, and obscure puns; yet each play has its own unity of mood and attitude.

Yūgen is an expression used in Chinese classics and Buddhist writings to signify fundamental, intuitively grasped depth of life. *Gen* is the dark principle of life of Laotse, *yū*, mysterious, being merely an explanatory and weakening adjective applied later. In the Japanese Middle Ages it was used by Fujiwara Shunzei concerning the ideal and inward beauty of *waka,* and employed gradually by other literary and artistic people. Zeami writes in his *Shikadō,* a chapter of his works other than the *Kadensho*: "A white bird holding a flower in its beak,—is not this the very form and pressure of *yūgen?*" When Bashō wished to express his "heart's desire" three hundred years later, he used precisely the opposite symbols, "a black crow perched on a withered branch." Zeami also has this *shibumi,* the restrained, the unobtrusive, the subdued, and we feel in him the contrast between the courtier and the free artist. He also renders unto Caesar the things that are Caesar's, the power, the beauty, and the glory; and renders unto God the things that are God's, the modesty and truth of nature. *Yūgen* is not mere beauty, such as we find in the *Genji Monogatari.* It has a purity that this masterpiece lacks. In the *Shikadō* but not in the *Kadensho,* I think, Zeami uses the word *ran-i* to denote a more abstract, more faded meaning of beauty than the word *yūgen,* closer in meaning to the *wabi* and *sabi* of Bashō. *Yūgen* and *ran-i* are part of Zen; they are the *satori* of art, the femaleness, the quietism of Zen, which has also the bleakness, the ruthlessness, the destructive violence of real life. What is the conclusion of all this? The problem is the connection between

Zen and Nō; was there a relation of cause and effect? Did Zen produce Nō? Or did the Zen of Nō appear spontaneously, unrelated to (Chinese) Zen practice and theory? As is always the case, rather than a pretended answer to a question, the important thing, and all that really matters, is to get the question clear. What is the relation of Nō to Zen? In the light of all that has been (unnecessarily?) already said, we may now restate the question: What is the relation between the value of Nō, that is, the Zen of Nō, and Zen? Clearly, the second "Zen" must refer to what was termed at the beginning of this essay, the Zen of timeless-activity-in-time. The Zen of Nō is indubitable. It comes in the poetry, in the Buddhist teaching and atmosphere (Zen is supposed to be the essence of Buddhism). It derives also from the fact that Kan-ami and Zeami were not only dramatic authors but actors; Zen is meaningful activity. The real question then is this: What is the relation of Nō to the Zen *sect,* and its no-teachings? And this is part of a larger problem: are the highest forms of culture (real culture is another name for Zen) related to historical Zen, the Zen which has its beginnings 3,000 years ago in the *Upanishads* and still continues in the works of Suzuki Daisetz? Does not Zen spontaneously appear in the choral preludes of Buxtehude, *Alice in Wonderland,* the paintings of Rousseau, the Nō plays? In all these it may not be possible to trace the devious and unsuspected routes by which the Zen of the *Upanishads* was carried to Asia and Europe via Buddhism and gnosticism and mysticism generally, but it seems probable in every case, as with *Cha no Yu* and *Ikebana* and *Bushidō,* that some external stimulus aroused that Zen which we must believe to be latent in every man. The doctrines of Zen were necessary to produce the doctrine-less Zen of the Nō plays.

But these two "Zens" are not really two. There is

no Zen in a principle or a dogma, but Zen is not wordless. There is no Zen in mere silence. Zen is meaning,
so that when silence and stillness really mean something, and voices and flutes and drums really mean
something, in any place, at any time, there is Zen.

ZEN AND ZEN

Shakespeare says:

> The lunatic, the lover, and the poet
> Are of imagination all compact.

The common feature of madness, love, and poetry is imagination, that is, Zen. Imagination is the power to create what already exists, and this power Shakespeare attributes to three types of persons only. It is natural and proper, therefore, that we should speak of Zen under these three aspects, that we should speak of it paradoxically, "lovingly," and poetically.

How is it that when we seek to express Zen intellectually, verbally, we are always landed in paradoxes and contradictions? The answer is simple: the intellect, like the dictionary, is dichotomous in its nature; it divides truth into two halves, and grasps one only of these halves,—which one being decided by the profit-or-loss principle. It is easy to say all this, but difficult really to understand it, for when we are stating a general principle we forget that this principle itself, however seemingly extensive in application, is only half the whole truth. The whole truth cannot, by definition, be stated in words, yet this very sentence is asserted in defiance of the definition. A common and obvious example is the much-used word "absolute," as against the relative. What is usually forgotten is that absolute is not the absolute absolute; it is the relative absolute, the absolute relative to the relative. As another example we may take the word "all." When we say "all," we think we include everything, but we do not; we exclude all that is not all. We omit the notion of not-all that is inevitably engendered when we cut into two the reality which includes all *and* not-all. In the

129

antagonism of science and religion, which is really that
of reason and intuition, we get the two halves of the
fact that everything, material or spiritual, is itself
alone, separate from every other, and at the same time
(not part, but) all things. Science aims at a unity
which is achieved in madness and mysticism, in love,
and in poetry, but it is not correct to speak of "Buddhahood, in which all the contradictions of the intellect
are entirely harmonised in a unity of a higher order,"
for Zen is harmony *and* disharmony. It is disunity just
as much as unity. When Shakespeare wrote *Hamlet,*
he became Hamlet. This is true, but at the same time
he remained Shakespeare, for without this paradoxical
condition no drama, no poetry, no *Hamlet,* is possible.

Zen is pretending. We pretend to be God, and make
the rain fall (when it does so). We pretend to be men,
and get wet. Ordinary people also pretend, but
alternately. The Zen pretending is pretending both at
the same instant. When Wordsworth killed Lucy, or
Shakespeare killed Desdemona, it was both murder and
suicide, but at the same time neither was a murderer,
neither took his own life.

The lunatic view of life, the lunatic life, includes not
only contradiction and paradox, but humour, "a feast
of unreason," which, according to Aristotle and Kant,
is founded upon contrast, upon the difference between
fact and fancy, real and ideal. But fancy is only a
different kind of fact, and the ideal is at least as real
as the real. Thus laughter is the result and the evidence
of the perception of the (intellectually contradictory)
whole truth. Again, humour or its invariable con-
comitant laughter—a laughter which may be visible and
audible, or not, but which is always physical—is not
a means, it is the end, enlightenment itself. The humour
of Zen is always implicit, sometimes explicit. For
example, in answer to the question "Why did Bodhidharma come to China?" that is, "What is the essence
of Zen?" the dozens of answers may be the opposite

to that expected by logic, or they may (appear to) be completely off the point and at random. But, to parody Pascal, "the intuition has its reasons which reason does not know of." Putting the matter less obscurely, a question and answer is always a half-question and a half-answer. The Zen answer may be the other half of the answer, or, better still, it may be the whole answer. When Jōshū was asked "Has this dog the Buddha-nature?" he answered "No!" This is the other-half answer, implying also the un-dichotomous nature of reality. When, however, Fuketsu was asked: "Both speaking and silence belong to the relative world: how can we escape from these two errors?" he answered:

> I always think of Kōnan in March;
> Partridges chirp among the scented blossoms.

This is not the realm of the absolute, nor is it that of the relative. To understand Jōshū's answer, we must remember the essence of the *Hannya Shingyō: Shiki soku ze kū, kū soku ze shiki. Shiki* means phenomena, the material world. *Kū* is the spiritual, what is often called reality. These two are not really two. To say they are one is perhaps going too far; if we say the (apparently) unreal and changing is no different from the real and the permanent, the relative is the absolute, we are repeating the notion of the sutra in other words, but Jōshū's words are not mere words. They are life being lived; they are the whole truth; they are the lunatic (and the lover and the poet) in action; they are silence speaking; they are of imagination all compact.

THE HISTORY OF ZEN IN THE WEST

Zen arises spontaneously, naturally, out of the human heart. It is not a special revelation to any person class, or nation. Thus to say it came from India to China and from China to Japan is nonsense. One might as well say that the air we breathe in one country comes from another. Further, the claim of Zen that it is "a special transmission," and that this line runs from Sakyamuni through the intervening twenty six patriarchs to Bodhidharma, Huike, Sengtsan, Taohisin, Hungjen, Huineng, down to the rōshi of the present day, is nothing but obscurantism, exclusivism, false patriotism, bigotry, pedantry, and egoism, in a word, the absence of the Zen spirit.

From the Zen, the poetical, the transcendental point of view, "never man spake such as he," is true of anybody, and in the last resort, of everybody, and our seeing the truth or not seeing it is a question of will; we will to see or will not to see, just as a crow wills to be black, and a snake wills its legs away.

Nevertheless there is after all a history of Zen in time. Cause and effect are just as real as they are unreal. If then we find the spirit of Zen in Homer, Epictetus, Plutarch, Marcus Aurelius, The Bible, *The Dream of Rood*, *The Inferno*, Eckhart's *Sermons*, *The Burning Babe*, *King Lear*, *Don Quixote*, Montaigne's *Essays*, the works of Bach and Mozart, *Animal Tranquillity and Decay*, *Auguries of Innocence*, Nietzsche, Clare's poetry, *A Week on the Concord*, *Martin Chuzzlewit*, Stevenson's *Fables*, we may properly search for historical relations, for a special transmission inside as well as outside the scriptures; we may depend on books and words, as we trace the connections between all these direct pointings to the soul of man, seeing into their

132

nature and attaining, even for a brief moment, Buddhahood.

Diogenes Laertius, writing about 230 A.D., says in his preface to *Lives of the Philosophers*:

> The Magi taught the Persians philosophy; the Chaldaeans taught it to the Babylonians and Assyrians; the Gymnosophists to the Indians; the Druids and Semnothei to the Gauls and Celts.

Philosophy means here what we should rather call religion; the order of the nations named does not imply any priority of time; there is no indication of the relation between them. In Plutarch's *Life of Alexander*, written 120 years before, he tells us of the meeting of Alexander with ten Gymnosophists when he reached the River Bias in India. He asked one of them which was first, the day or the night. He answered, "The day was first, by one day," and added, "Impossible questions require impossible answers." Another he asked how a man could make himself most beloved and was answered, "By being very powerful, and yet not feared by his subjects." A third, on being asked which was stronger, life or death, replied, "Life, because it endures such terrible sufferings."

These gymnosophists were famous for their "short pithy answers," and though these particular men may not have been Buddhist monks, they may have been something even better. In any case, such teachings, inculcating strong gentleness, practicality, brevity of utterance, universal benevolence, and obedience to the "reason" within and without men, were being spread not only to China but to the Near East by Buddhist missionaries. Such a mission, before 230 B.C., is reported to have been sent to Ptolemy of Egypt, King Antiochus of Syria, and others, in the inscriptions of King Asoka. In Greece the Cynics reproduce and perhaps imitate the Buddhist monks. Epictetus describes Diogenes, "a man who has nothing, who is naked, houseless, without a hearth, squalid, without a slave, without a city." The Buddhists influenced the Essenes perhaps, and through them Christ, Christianity, and the Christian world.

The Stoics believed, with the Buddhists, in the freedom of man and the dominion of fate, in the non-dualism of the absence of the principle of evil, and the Stoics, themselves affected by Judaism and Persian thought, influenced Christianity, not only in the doctrine of the Logos, the worship of Wisdom, and the Buddhistic Sermon on the Mount, but the ideals, the discipline, and the morality of Christian society. Thus the idealistic practicality of Zeno has made Europe far more poetical, more true, more Zen-like, than the abstractions of Plato or the rationality of Aristotle.

The Cynic school, founded by Antisthenes, the favourite pupil of Socrates, is more like Zen in its teachings than the Stoic. Their lives were as simple and self-renouncing as that of Zen monks. They were philosophical anarchists, and anarchistic philosophers; they did not believe in Plato's forms, but only in things. They could have guessed part of the meaning of "The Buddha is three pounds of flax." They believed in intuition, in acting upon the impulse of each moment. They were apparently anti-social, and worshipped liberty. It seems strange, when one thinks of it, that the Greek Cynics did not create Zen, and the Chinese Buddhists did. The reasons must be first, the national spirit, which in the Greeks is wordy, in the Chinese laconic. Or to put the matter more exactly, in Greece as in China, there were both intellectual and intuitive types, but in Greece the former greatly preponderated. The Chinese had no sophists, of any ability, that is, to make the worse seem the better reason. Second, the Greeks were social in a larger sense than the Chinese, and the very universality of the Greek notions militated against the perception of infinity in a grain of sand and eternity in an hour, *never leaving the grain of sand and the hour*. Third, the special characteristic of (Chinese) Zen is the establishment of (religious) non-sense as the cause and test of enlighten-

ment. The Greeks could not for a moment give up
their heads, their rational questions and rational answers. The Chinese, if it is not too rude to say so, had
no heads from the beginning, and the same may be
said of the Japanese, who have always hated logic and
psychology, and perhaps always will. The Greeks were
men, the Chinese and Japanese were women, and
women are always more right than men.

Diogenes Laertius tells us how Crates, who wore
warm clothes in summer and rags in winter, and
entered the theatre when the play was over, was loved
by Hipparchia, who gave up all her wealth to live
with him. Here again we see the difference between
the Chinese and the Greeks. Chinese eccentrics are
many, but they are always solitary. Zen is indeed a
selfish and Hinayana religion, for all its Mahayana
professions.

Each citizen of Zeno's ideal state is a citizen of the
world. There are no laws, no temples, no statues, no
Olympics. Men and women wear the same dress, and
do not hide their bodies. The dead are buried in the
earth, or burned, or exposed, indifferently. This is the
Zen of Zeno, who taught that soul is body and body
is soul. God is pure body. The Logos is the deity.
These propositions Chinese Zen would not oppose, but
it would not accept the syllogisms of Zeno, and in this
respect the instinct of Zen was correct. For example,
"No evil is accompanied by glory; but death is accompanied by glory; therefore death is no evil." It is true
that intuition and reason must attain the same truth
by their different roads, but reason itself is based on
intuitions which need to be tested as to their depth,
permanence, and invariability.

Cleanthes, Zeno's most faithful disciple, who became
head of the school even before Zeno's death, was a
man who lived a life of Zen, reminding us of Yenyuan,
Confucius best disciple. He worked as a water-drawer
at night so that he might study philosophy by day,
and wrote in verse so as to teach the common people,

who could perhaps easily understand his best known
saying, "The fates lead us willing, unwilling, drag us."
Chrysippus, born 280 B.C., took Stoicism farther from
the intuitionalism of Cynicism and made it still more
logical, that is, more dualistic, that is, less Zen-like.

The founder of Roman Stoicism was Panaetius, but
it is a watered-down, gentlemanly thing, with the
paradoxes weakened, and decorum taking the place of
the courage of Cynicism and the wisdom of (Greek)
Stoicism. The soul and the body are once more divided,
as in the Persian religion. Attalus, the teacher of
Cicero, taught poverty as an intrinsic value. Far more
than the vulgar and feeble Seneca, his contemporary
Musonius gives us somewhat of the feeling of a Zen
monk in his disdain of applause and independent,
accusing attitude. One of his most famous maxims is:
"Live each day as if your last!" When the armies of
Vespasian and Vitellius were fighting in the suburbs
of Rome, just after Nero's death, Musonius addressed
the ordinary soldiers on the virtues of pacifism. He
was manhandled, but not killed. There are no such
anecdotes in the history of Chinese or Japanese Zen.

In the second century A.D. appear two great Stoics,
Epictetus and Marcus Aurelius. The former has some
energy of thought and a feeling of social responsibility
which Zen lacked, for example, "You came into
existence, not when you chose, but when the world
had need of you." Marcus Aurelius is after all an
emperor, an imperialist also in religion:

> If indeed the Gods take no thought for anything
> at all—an impious creed—then let us have done with
> sacrifice and prayer and oaths, and all other
> observances by which we own the presence and the
> nearness of the Gods.

(It should be noted that being an emperor distorts the
mind,—*but so does not being an emperor*.) The sad
thoughts of Marcus Aurelius on death are not Christian,
not Buddhist, not even Zen:

Serenely you await the end, be it extinction or transmutation. While the hour yet tarries, what help is there? What, but to reverence and bless the gods, to do good to men, "to endure and to refrain"? And of all that lies outside the bounds of flesh and breath, to remember that it is not yours, nor in your power.

These tones are heard in Wordsworth's

> My hopes must no more change their name;
> I long for a repose that ever is the same.

The decadence of Rome and the decadence of England follow the same pattern. Zen is non-decadence.

The mistake of the Stoics was their adherence to the doctrine of the validity of the intellect alone to be the instrument of the discovery or creation of truth. They saw clearly that the world is ruled by fate, they believed also in human freedom and responsibility, but were not willing to state both boldly, as being both 100% true. The Chinese, on the other hand, could answer "It has," and "It hasn't," to the question "Has a dog the Buddha nature?" meaning, "Yes it has if it has, and it hasn't if it hasn't." They learned this from the Indians, who could say, "Yes, it hasn't if it has," or, "No, it has if it hasn't," rising above the dichotomy of logic, or rather, using words with a Zen connotation. The Greeks escaped occasionally from logic in paradox or in poetry, but reason was almost always too strong for them. The Chinese had little or none, the Japanese littler or noner.

Before treating of another great flow of thought, mysticism, it might be well to think back to a much earlier example of Zen, found in art, which almost certainly antedates music and literature, perhaps even speech. The cave-paintings of the Pyrenees and South-Western France are at once religious and artistic. They are a culminating point in the history of mankind thousands of years ago. Where literature or art or music or human actions are at their best, there is Zen. We may, we must expect to find some sort of Zen in these cave paintings. There is religious awe, aesthetic value, and a co-fulfilment of the physical needs of the artist-priests and their audience. There is an imagination which sees into the life of the animal, and relates it to the life of human beings.

When goodness truth and beauty are all present, as one, there is Zen. In many of these paintings on the walls of almost inaccessible caves, in impenetrable darkness, seen only by the doubtful light of torches in smoky air that could not be breathed long, men who were more really human than ourselves saw once more with their hands the animals they had seen with their eyes in the bright world outside. To live, to kill, to eat, to be one with things, to see things as they are, to see them as they ought to be, to know the real and the ideal, to grasp movement in stillness, and stillness in movement,—to do all this was what they did, and to do all this is Zen. What is interesting is that most of the animals are shown in repose, or swimming or running, or grazing; only a few are killed, or being killed. To want a thing for its own sake, not for my sake, this is Zen, yet after all your sake is my sake, and my sake is just a long way round (several hundred million years of human history) to your sake and its sake. Thus in the last resort, use and value, happiness and blessedness, means and ends, the eating of animals with the mouth and with the (inner) eye are the same. Yet they are different, and when the two are 100% the same and 100% different, there is ZEN.

Stoicism was an approach to Zen through morality. When morality generalises and becomes abstract it goes far from Zen. The danger inherent in mysticism is the same. In the end it becomes vast, vague, inane. Everything is dissolved in God or in Nature. Zen never for a moment loses touch with the particular, the concrete, the thingness of things, and for that reason we may call the cave art of the Paleolithic period Zen, though mysticism was already present, and our writing about this art and about Zen is itself an example of the intellectualising, the fossilisation, the starving of Zen, that is, of life, of material-meaning.

Mysticism is the state of union, of re-union of a person with the impersonal. This union is only possible, of course, if the person is impersonal, and the impersonal is personal. This is part of the meaning of the Tendai philosophy of the Three Thousand Worlds, all of which penetrate each other, so that a man keeps a stony silence, and a stone looks cold, God is angry, and we forgive him; a tree sighs its bosom over us, and Hell is in Heaven and Heaven not outside Hell.

The etymology of the words mysticism and Zen brings out clearly the difference between these truly similar states of mind and forms of life. Mysticism seems to be derived from the Greek word *muein*, to keep one's mouth shut, and as with the pagan Mysteries, the Christian mystic was told "not to utter or divulge the heavenly mysteries unto the uninitiate" (Dionysius, *The Divine Names* 1,8.). In Zen this sort of thing is impossible. We can say what mysticism is, but no one has ever said or will ever say what Zen is. In fact the expression of Zen is more mysterious than silence about it, for silence might be regarded as not saying what could be said, but to pull a man's nose, or say "Kwatz!" or merely to repeat the question,—how can these do anything more than increase the observer's confusion?

Zen derives historically to a great extent from the spiritual experiences of the Indian race during the first millenium before Christ, for example, the last words of the *Taittireeya Upanishad*:

> I am this world, and I eat this world.
> Who knows this, knows.

This expresses, or records, a state of mind in which, first, there is no division between I and not-I. The relation of myself to the universe is not a problem, intellectual or emotional, because *I am it*. There is no good and evil, true and untrue, beautiful and ugly, enlightenment and illusion. Second, this state is not a passive, but an active one, a state of eating, a perpetual Holy Communion of eating one's own body and drinking one's own blood. In other words, the whole affair is interesting; I enjoy *myself*.

This experience was repeated again and again in (later) time and (a different) place, that is to say, it was carried from India to China, to Korea, to Japan, the carrier being Buddhism, a non-religious, atheistical, intellectual, unpoetical system which nevertheless could provide the innocuous and necessary moral and philosophical framework within which the poetico-religious life could develop.

In the same way it was intellectual Hellenism which was the rational basis of the supra-rational mystical intuitions of Plotinus, the father of Christian mysticism though himself not a Christian. His transcendentalism he derived partly from Plato, partly from the Egyptian, Greek, and Roman mysteries, but there can be no doubt that Indian and Persian thought influenced him and his contemporaries greatly. Plotinus must have met many Indian travellers in Alexandria, his native place, and wanted to get first-hand information upon Indian mysticism. For this reason he endeavoured to reach India by accompanying the army of the Emperor Gordian against the Persians in 244 A.D. However. the Emperor was assassinated, and Plotinus was forced to turn back from Mesopotamia, and arrived in Rome late the same year. The fact that Plotinus does not mention India or Indian philosophy in his works shows nothing, for he does not say anything about the Christianity by which he was surrounded, nor does he mention his teacher Ammonius Saccus from whom he learned for eleven years, until he was thirty nine. This probable historical connection between Zen and mysticism, corresponding to that between Bashō and Wordsworth, explains the similarities between them. (Thoreau is even closer to Bashō than Wordsworth, this being again partly due to the Indian writings

which he received from an English friend, and which
gave him that philosophic background needed for all
poetical and religious experiences.) The differences
between Bashō and Wordsworth are those between the
Chinese-Japanese mind and the German-English mind,
the latter always moving from the particular to the
universal, the concrete to the abstract, the former
never leaving the particular and the concrete however
much the universal and abstract may be implicit in
them. In a sense, Zen and Bashō are better (that is,
deeper) than mysticism and Wordsworth, but we do
not really *know* this, in other words, it is not actually
so, until we have studied occidental philosophy and
poetry.

From the above point of view, Zen and Mysticism
may be said to form a bridge, both historical and
spiritual, between Occident and Orient. Indeed the
Japanese educational system might well be aligned to
it. We have India as the chief fountain of world culture;
the two streams running east and west, the eastern
with its Chinese and Japanese art, poetry, and religion;
the western and its Italian art, German mysticism and
music, English poetry.

Neoplatonism entered Christianity through St.
Augustine, who lived two centuries after Plotinus.
The Neoplatonic school was closed by the Emperor
Justinian a century after the death of Augustine, but
its influence on European literature was profound, continuous, and permanent. Eriugena, the great 9th century Irish theologian, translated "Dionysius" from
Greek into Latin. This Dionysius the Areopagite
introduced oriental mysticism directly into Roman-
Jewish Christianity, and brought about the Christian
mysticism of such persons as Hugh of St. Victor, 1096-
1141, and thus ultimately produced Eckhart, 1260-1327,
the greatest of all mystics and mystical writers. Ficino,
1433-1499, studied Plotinus deeply, and spread his
"doctrines" throughout Europe, but rather than the
published work of the scholars and the writings of

the saints, such as John Hylton and Juliana of Norwich, there was an underflow, a more popular and debased form of mysticism, mixes with magic and alchemy and theurapy, that produced, purified by their own character, the writings of Boehme and Vaughan and Blake, and Wordsworth (through Coleridge). Emerson and Thoreau went back to Plotinus, and found in him a support and justification of their intuitions and experiences, but the Zen we find in all these more or less Christian mystics comes down from Egypt, Greece, and Persia, ultimately from India. The most ordinary saying of the poets often derive from unexpectedly far-off places. Wordsworth's lines,

> O cuckoo, shall I call thee Bird,
> Or but a wandering Voice?

comes from the ancient, pre-Christian doctrine of the Logos. As for the following,—who can trace the remote origins of the Zen in them?

> Life is a pure flame, and we live by any invisible sun within us.

> Silence was pleased.

> It is the stars,
> The stars above, govern our conditions.

> Eternity was in our lips and eyes.

> In great haste I am sent to thee
> From God out of his majesty.

> Ah Sunflower, weary of time,
> That countest the steps of the sun!

> We worship God best when we resemble Him most.

> I must kill him,
> And I will do it bravely: the mere joy
> Tells me, I merit in it.

But when we take Chinese or Japanese writings, it is equally difficult to know their remote origins:

> The name that can be named is not an eternal name.

My abode has no pillars; it is roofless,—Yet the rain does not wet it, nor the wind strike it.

Don't be afraid of blinking when the eye unexpectedly confronts an object; it is natural.

> Rain running down
> A paulownia tree
> Under the belly of a cicada.

> No target set up,
> No bow drawn,
> And the arrow leaves the string;
> It may not hit,
> But it will not miss!

In all Heaven and Earth, there is no scene of beauty.

> Blooming, and then scattering,
> And leaving all to rain and wind,—
> The cherry-blossoms are no more!
> But their spirit remains for ever undisturbed.

Tea is Tea only when Tea is No-tea.

> If your ears see,
> And your eyes hear,
> Not a doubt you will cherish,—
> And how naturally the rain drops
> From the eaves!

Asceticism, "cynicism," "stoicism," animism, mysticism, humour,—these suggest the presence of Zen, just as do unconventionality, naturalness, understatement, freedom, in Western as in Eastern life and literature and art. But at the same time, as said before, there is a double flow dimly discernible in the history of humanity, in the history of humanness, from India to China and Japan, and from India to Greece-Persia-Egypt and Europe. The rate of flow was different, not merely as a result of geography, but because Greece especially and Europe also had "to overcome the world," the world in this case being the world of the pure intellect, of which the (Far) East knew little.

FOUR JAPANESE MONKS

The Japanese have no genius for religion, in the ordinary sense of the word. They can drink tea religiously, arrange flowers religiously, write poetry, paint pictures, build shrines religiously, even kill people religiously and go to the lavatory religiously, but they can't be just religious. In a church or a temple they look and feel hypocrites and dastards. Thus, when we consider the four greatest Japanese Zen monks, Ikkyu, 1394-1481, Takuan, 1573-1645, Hakuin, 1685-1768, and Ryōkan, 1758-1831, (I omit Dōgen, because I think him infatuated, incoherent, and unlovable) we must not look for anything like we find in Wumen or Linchi. The trenchancy of the Chinese changes to the softness of the Japanese, the solid becomes liquid. Thus it is better to begin with Ryōkan, not because he is necessarily the greatest, but because I think that if we can understand Ryōkan we understand all the rest of them; he provides us with both an example and a standard. Ryōkan is not to be found in *Zenshu Jiten,* the Dictionary of Zen, or in the great Buddhist Dictionaries, but appears quite prominently in Japanese literature and in the history of calligraphy. Indeed, not knowing otherwise, one would suppose that he belonged rather to the *tariki* side of Buddhism, to Jōdoshū or Shinshū than to Zenshū, and it is precisely this anti-social or rather non-social aspect of Ryōkan which is most interesting. However, it is not the scorn of the world of Tao Yunming or Yoshida Kenkō that we find in him. Ryōkan felt himself to be inferior, not superior, to ordinary people, and this was not due to any inferiority complex, but to the fact that he was, in fact, inferior to them, in everything but self-knowledge. He was actually a kind of fool and it was for this reason partly that he became a monk and lived by himself.

When I was young, like all other English children I read *Robinson Crusoe*. But I think I read it more often, more earnestly than other boys. It was not that I wanted to visit strange lands and lead a life of danger and adventure,—far from it. It was the idea of living alone like John Clare or Wordsworth, better still, like the old Chinese and Japanese hermits, such as Hanzan or Chōmei. In a way it is a kind of cowardice, a kind of stupidity which brings about this desire, but the desire itself is for nature and poetry and loneliness. And in this physical cowardice and inability "to see the causes of things" there is a spiritual value which the Napoleons and Nietzsches of this world overlook. Sōma Gyofū, who has not only written many books about Ryōkan but really understands him, calls one of them *The Great Fool Ryōkan,* and this word "fool," if we grasp the significance of it, is the key to Ryōkan's life, and to his value as a human being. In the first chapter of the first *Epistle to the Corinthians*, Paul approaches to this meaning of foolishness, particularly in verse twenty five, where he says, "The foolishness of God is wiser than men; and the weakness of God is stronger than men." During the Middle Ages fools were much appreciated in Europe, and the fool in *King Lear* approximates, in his weakness, pathos, truthfulness, and understanding of the tragic nature of human life, to Ryōkan. But unlike the fool in *Lear*, Ryōkan had no desire to teach royalty its duties. Being himself a child of God, a child of Buddha, a child of nature, Ryōkan was in his element with children:

子供らと手たづさえて春の野に
若菜をつめばたのしくあるかな

Kodomora to te tazusaete haru no no ni
Wakana wo tsumeba tanoshiku aru kana

How happy I am
As I go hand in hand
With the children,

> To gather young greens
> In the fields of spring !

He often reproached himself, but never for his way of life. He did not hold up either, however, as a model for others. Each man, Ryōkan probably thought, must (and anyway does) live according to his own nature. The only thing is, what is this particular man's nature? What is my, your nature? Is it the same? Is it the so-called "Buddha-nature"? Hardly, because this would involve a dreadful uniformity, and in any case each man is to act freely from himself, not according to some philosophical theory of a general, abstract, universal nature. Indeed, it is not so much "the world's coarse thumb" as that of learning, of morality, of formal religion that fails to plumb the mind of Ryōkan. A poor weak creature who did nothing for mankind but lived a life as humble as that of woodlouse,—how is it that this simpleton, this simple Simon can touch our hearts so deeply in this age of power and pride of service? He did not, like Thoreau, work even three days a week:

焚くほどに風がもてくる落葉かな

Taku hodo ni kaze ga mote kuru ochiba kana

> The wind brings enough
> Of fallen leaves
> To make a fire.

We may wish to think of him as an artist, as a poet, as (what he was) a great calligrapher, but he himself says:

> There are three things I dislike: poems by a poet, handwriting by an artist, and food by a cook.

Ryōkan never preached, never tried to push anyone into Heaven. Like Christ in Lawrence's *The Man Who Died,* he could say, "The teacher and saviour are dead in me." He never did any good deeds, and lived freely as he wished, yet he was admired and beloved by all the villagers. No one wanted to poison or crucify him

On the one hand the life of Ryōkan was that of quietness and purity, and it had its profound pleasure, just like that of Wordsworth at the cry of the cuckoo, or the sight of the glow-worm:

草の庵に足さしのべて小山田の
山田の蛙きくがたのしさ

*Kusa no io ni ashi sashinobete koyamada no
yamada no kawazu kikuga tanoshisa*

> What a happy thing it is
> To listen to the frogs
> In the mountain fields,
> Stretched at full length
> In my thatched hut!

But on the other hand, he could not forget the misery of the times, the decay of the Military Government of the Tokugawa, the decadence of people, the suicide of his own father, the vulgarity, the scoffing (even senryu itself was now degenerating). He could not help grieving for the world outside:

思うまじ思うまじとは思えども
思いだしては袖しをるなり

*Omoumaji omoumaji to wa omoedomo
omoidashite wa sode shioru nari*

> Though I think
> Not to think about it any more,
> I do think about it,
> And wet my sleeves
> Thinking about it.

What a warm, simple, tender heart he has! This love for others is not willed, it is not cultivated; it is not self-conscious or artificial. It springs from his choosing this solitary and lonely life, in which his intuitions became deeper and purer and clearer. As Emerson says,

> When the half-gods go,
> The gods arrive.

If we are attached to nothing, because all things are shed like the leaves of autumn, then naturally our feelings overflow onto others, and we "bless them unawares." And this compassion includes also ourselves:

山住みのあわれを誰に語らまし
まれ見にも人の来ても訪はねば

Yamazumi no aware wo dare ni kataramashi
mare mi ni mo hito no kite mo towaneba

Whom can I tell
Of the loneliness of life
In the mountains,
If people come not see me,
Even sometimes?

As he grew older his soul became more lucid (full of light) more selfless, more unseparated from nature, more serene. His last poem:

形見とて何か残さん春は花
夏時鳥秋はもみじ葉

Katami tote nani ka nokosan haru wa hana
natsu hototogisu aki wa momijiba

What shall I leave
As a memento?
Flowers in the spring,
The *hototogisu* in summer,
Tinted leaves of autumn.

This reminds us of Wordsworth's lines at the end of *The Education of Nature:*

She died, and left to me
This heath, this calm and quiet scene.

We see then that Ryōkan was after all living by the Zen that he never spoke about, never even thought of. He lived in Zen just as the fish lives in the water or the bird in air. To the good, goodness is invisible; to the truthful (in action) there is no truth and untruth to be contrasted to each other, nor to be equated Ryōkan could have said as Thoreau did on his deathbed when asked if he had made his peace with God:

"I have never quarrelled with Him." Ryōkan had much in common also with Hanzan, the Chinese hermit, but closest of all is the man described by Wordsworth in *A Poet's Epitaph:*

> He is retired as noon-tide dew,
> Or fountain in a noon-day grove;
> And you must love him, ere to you
> He will seem worthy of your love.

> But he is weak; both Man and Boy,
> Hath been an idler in the land;
> Contented if he might enjoy
> The things which others understand.

Hakuin

The most interesting thing about Hakuin is not the doubtful anecdotes told of him, his Buddhist doctrines, his rules for health, but his actual life. In his tenacity of purpose (to get *satori*), his sincerity, and self-confidence, he reminds us of the greatest Chinese Zen monks, but there is a certain lack of what we may call breadth of mind, that prevents us from calling him great. It is not enough to say that he lived in a feudalistic age, in a country which had cut itself off from the rest of the world. Bashō was his contemporary, but there is nothing narrow, insular, superstitious, or pedantic about the founder of the Way of Haiku. Yet we must remember that, without the Zen which such men as Hakuin discovered-created, Bashō would have been but a poetaster, a mere dilettant.

Hakuin, the founder of the Rinzai sect of Zen in Japan, was born in 1683 (Bashō died in 1684). From his earliest years he had an extreme dread of Hell. By the time he was twelve years old he wanted to become a priest, but was not allowed to until he was fourteen. At fifteen he studied the *Hokke Kyō* assiduously, but found no religious meaning in this sutra and despised it; this he was to regret in later life. When he was nineteen he travelled about the country seeking en-

lightenment. One of the things he could not understand was the murder of Gantō (Yen-tou), 828-887,
a great Tang Zen master. It was said that the screams
of his death agony were heard for miles around.
Gantō's gruesomely inappropriate death troubled
Hakuin's mind constantly, and for some time he gave
up Zen and practised calligraphy and studied Chinese
poetry. When he was twenty-three years old he had
his first *satori,* while meditating on Jōshu's *Mu.* He
tells us in his book *ORategama* how he heard a distant
temple bell which upset his intellectual pack of cards
completely. He realised that he himself was Gantō,
though with no diminution whatever of his own personality; that there was no birth-and-death to escape
from, and no supreme wisdom to strive for.

We now come to the most interesting episode of
Hakuin's life, his second enlightenment at the hands
(rather literally) of Shōju Rōjin. When Hakuin visited
him he saw at a glance his satori-conceit. He said to
him, "What you have *learned* is in this verse you have
given me, but what have you *seen*?" Hakuin replied,
"If I had something to show, I would spit it out!" and
he made the motions of vomiting. Shōju struck him,
then asked his opinion of Joshu's *Mu.* Hakuin said he
had nowhere to put his arms and legs while he looked
at it. Shōju said with a sneer, "You seem to know
something about where to put arms and legs!" cuffed
him, and from that time on called him, "You devil in
a dark cave!" Hakuin was non-plussed, but began to
realise that his Zen was *Zen-kusai,* it stank of Zen,
when Zen should smell of nothing, or of everything.

One day Hakuin was begging at the door of a house.
The woman refused him, but Hakuin was in a kind of
trance and did not move. She refused again, and still
he did not move. The woman, evidently short-tempered,
or having, like many women, a grudge against men in
general, caught him a wallop over the head with her
broom. Hakuin fell unconscious, but when he revived,
he was a different man indeed, and how joyfully Shōju

received him! His eight months of bracing by damning
had not been in vain.

Hakuin contracted consumption through incessant
asceticism and zazen, but managed to cure himself
within three years by what we would now call mental
healing. His principle was that the mind must fill every
part of the body, every hair and pore, not a single spot
left vacant for disease to enter.

Once Hakuin did zazen for seven days and nights
without sleeping. He records his *satori* on this occasion
by a very good waka. (It should be noted that the
"sounds" of the snow is the muffled thud of the snow
falling from the trees or the roofs.)

> How I would like people to hear
> In the old temple
> Of the forests of Shinoda
> These sounds of snow falling
> Through the deepening night!

From the age of 31 he lived in his old home at
Shōinji Temple near Mount Fuji. When he first went
there, "the stars shone through [the roofs] at night,
nor were there any proper floors. If it was raining, it
was necessary to have a rain-hat and high geta when
anything was going on in the main part of the temple."
But things improved, and as the place was on the
Tōkaidō, he was visited by many people of high and
low rank. He taught all according to their position,
speaking to Lords of mercy, to samurai of death, to
officials of simplicity of life, to farmers of karma, to
servants of obedience.

In 1768, when he was 83 years old, he fell ill; refusing
doctors he became worse, groaned, and died. There is
something fitting in the manner of his death.

What is striking and characteristic about Hakuin is
the way in which he insists upon *satori* as the aim of
life. *Satori* is the pearl of great price, and a man must
sell all that he has to get it. In this, in his extreme
asceticism, and in what he says about the joy of enlightenment, he reminds us of the sixteenth century

Spanish mystic St. John of the Cross, who "gave his body no rest," but who says in *The Ascent of Mount Carmel,*

Such is the sweetness of deep delight of these touches of God, that one of them is more than a recompense for all the sufferings of this life, however great their number.

Hakuin, in *Orategama,* speaks of satori as

an event accompanied with a feeling of immense joy such as never before experienced in one's life.

This joy is not at the fact that enlightenment has been gained, nor is it the satisfaction that "a crown is laid up for me in Heaven," but joy, as Hakuin says at the beginning of his *Song of Meditation,* that

All sentient beings are from the beginning Buddhas,

and once more at the end, that

This very earth is the Lotus Land of Purity,
And this body the body of the Buddha.

Hakuin does not touch our hearts as Ryōkan does; he touches something deeper, the soul with its everspringing desire for truth, that living truth without which we feel we shall have lived and loved and laughed and wept in vain.

Takuan

Takuan, born in 1573, lived through the most exciting period of Japanese history, the "reigns" of the first three Shōguns, Ieyasu, Hidetada, and Iemitsu. But sixteenth and seventeenth century Japan was no different from any other place or time:

If we follow the world, we turn our backs on the Way. If we do not turn our backs on the Way, we do not follow the world,

says Takuan in *Tōkaiyawa,* and the first part of his

life was spent in austerities and penetrating into the
open secrets of Zen. He learned also Confucianism and
the writing of Chinese poetry from Bunsai.

In 1669, when he was 37 years old, he became Master
of the famous temple Daitokuji, where Oda Nobunaga
was buried, but soon after retired, leaving a poem
saying that he was by nature a wandering monk and
could not live in a splendid cage in the capital. From
this time he led a retired life until he was 56 (1628)
spending much time in writing, and rebuilding some
famous Zen temples here and there. He tells us of
himself in *Tōkaiyawa*:

> I never feel lonely. When a visitor goes back, I
> feel how nice and quiet it is. And when dusk falls
> I think, "Nobody can come now, I can be by myself.
> The moon and the rain are also alone and quiet, and
> I feel them to be my rain, my moon."

All this sounds romantic and sentimental but Takuan
goes on to explain that this is not his state of mind.
He says he is not seeking aesthetic or ascetic pleasure;
he is simply acting according to his own nature. To
seek pleasure in nature and loneliness would be no
different from seeking for it in dissipation and society.

However, something occurred which caused his
banishment. Up to this time it was the Emperor who
appointed the head priest of Daitokuji Temple (built
in 1323 by Daitō Kokushi, and made famous by Ikkyū
in the 15th century) but Ieyasu wanted to get all power
into his own hands. He died before he was able to do
this. The Second Shōgun made the qualifications for
office so difficult that Takuan and other priests sent
in a representation to the Shōgun, for which he was
banished to Ushū from 1625 to 1632. The Emperor
Gomizunoo abdicated in anger. However, the 3rd Shōgun, Iemitsu, admired and liked Takuan, and built him
Tōkaiji Temple to keep him in Edo.

When on his death-bed, in 1645, he was asked to
write a death poem. He refused, but at last wrote the
character *Yume*, Dream, and died. One year before

this another great man had been born, Bashō, who at the end of his life wrote a death poem using the same character:

> Ill on a journey,
> My dreams wander
> Over a withered moor.

Takuan's will is interesting; it might have been written by Bernard Shaw:

> Bury my body in the mountain behind the temple. Just cover it with soil and go away. Do not read any sutras; do not make an altar; do not receive obituary gifts. The clothes and the meals of the priests should be as usual. Do not ask for a posthumous title. Do not erect a tomb-stone, or make a wooden mortuary tablet. Do not write my life story.

What Takuan wanted was to deny himself, Takuan, in history, so as to affirm the Way. In one of his writings, *Ketsujōshū*, he says that we will have no troubles if we think we come into this world as guests. As guests we must praise the meal, even if we do not like it. We must put up with the heat of summer, the coldness of winter. We must be on good terms with our children and brothers and sisters, who are fellow guests. In a waka he says:

> Invited by our parents,
> We came here
> As temporary guests,
> And without remaining mind,
> We go back to our native place.

Takuan composed waka, kyōka (mad poems), utai (Nō plays), made renka (linked poems), wrote on gardening, the Art of Tea, but he is noted for two not very connected things, a way of pickling radishes named after him Takuan-zuke; and the application of Zen to the Art of Fencing, fencing in this case meaning the art of killing other people with a sword. Takuan was himself a living example of that famous line in the *Diamond Sutra,* one of the great sentences

A Landscape, by Takuan

The inscription, by the painter, is:

聽心不聽耳，茅屋個無声，暗識舟中客，瀟湘一夜情。

I listen with my mind, not with my ears,
And on the poor roof, the rain is soundless to me.
I can guess the feelings
Of the voyagers at Hsiaohsiang at night.

The picture is a scene of rain at Hsiaohsiang, a
famous meeting-place of two rivers. Takuan seems
to be thinking of some incident which occurred there.

of the world, which caused the satori of Enō the sixth
Patriarch, and led to all that is best in Japanese culture,

応無所住而生其心

O mu sho jū ni shō go shin,

Arouse the mind without fixing it anywhere.

Takuan applied this to the art of the warrior,
whose aim was to kill his enemy. He says at the
beginning of *Fudōchishinmyoroku,* Record of Divine
Immovable Intelligence:

> *Fudō* means not to move, but not as a lifeless stone
> or tree. *Fudōchi,* immovable wisdom, means to move
> here and there, right and left, in every direction
> wherever the mind wants to, without its stopping on
> and clutching any one object.... When you are
> going to be struck by an enemy's sword, if you put
> your mind on it, your activity is thwarted and you
> will be killed by him.... If you do not attach your
> mind to the sword or its movement or some plan or
> theory of fighting, you can turn the opponents'
> sword in his direction and kill *him.*

What is wrong with what Takuan writes about fighting is not the killing; murder, as De Quincey says, is
one of the fine arts. The defect lies in the over-
insistence upon winning. Properly enough, we want
to win, but Zen is not how to win; it is how to win or
lose. But rather than end on this note of criticism,
let me quote one of Takuan's best waka, seemingly at
the other extreme of attack and defence, but not really
so, if it is not to taken sentimentally, but absolutely:

心だに真の道に入るならば祈らずとても神や守らむ

Kokoro da ni makoto no michi ni iru naraba
Inorazu totemo kami ya mamoran

> If we walk
> The true Way
> In our inmost heart,
> Even without praying,
> God will be with us.

Ikkyū

Ikkyū Zenji is the most remarkable monk in the
history of Japanese Buddhism, the only Japanese com-
parable to the great Chinese Zen masters, for example,
Jōshu, 778-897; Rinzai, d. 867; Unmon, d. 996. But he
is different from these, and from all the other Zen
Masters in that he does not deny, by his silence, the
existence of sex. Just as the moon does not make a
hole in the water, so enlightenment, real enlightenment, does not rid a man of his human nature. Thoreau
says in his *Journals,* 1857, "I see that the infidels and
skeptics have formed themselves into churches, and
weekly gather together at the ringing of a bell." Ikkyū
is as free of Zen and zazen and the 1700 koans as
Thoreau is of churches and church-going and dogmas,
and thus has no position in the so-called "History of
Zen." Ikkyū reminds us also of the 19th century clergy-
man Sydney Smith, in his being anti-priest, careless
of dignity, and a believer in the saving power of
humour. He is unlike Bashō or Ryōkan; he has no
"quietness" in him, and inclines to vulgarity. Ikkyū
is closest to the Zen priest Sengai, 1750-1837, who also
associated with all classes of society, and painted some
of the best Zenga (Zen pictures) in existence. The
real Ikkyū is difficult to grasp; there is a pureness that
is elusive, a lack of back and front which escapes our
paradoxes. He is indeed the cloud in the sky, the foam
on the water, the shadow of the bamboo on the palace
steps, the sound of the wind in the picture.

Ikkyū was born on New Year's Day 1394, six years
before the death of Chaucer, his mother being a Lady
in Waiting to the Emperor Go-Komatsu, the 100th
Emperor of Japan. She seems to have waited too much
or too long on various occasions, and became pregnant,
thus incurring the displeasure (so it is said) of the
Empress, who had her dismissed. When he was in his
twenties he heard of Kasō Zenji in Katada, endeavoured

to enter his temple, and at last succeeded in doing so.
Kasō's temple was in a very poor condition, the food
being rather less than the minimum to sustain life.
When food and clothing ran out completely, Ikkyū
would go to Kyōto, make some incense, sell it, and
come back with the pittance thus gained. Six years
passed in a sort of duel between the sullen teacher
and the desperate novice. In the evening of the 20th
of May, 1420, Ikkyū became enlightened on hearing
the caw of a crow. In 1428 Kasō died; Ikkyū was now
34. Kasō had given him a certificate of his enlightenment, but Ikkyū only threw it on the ground. Kasō
wrote another, and later, this document fell into his
hands, and he shed tears as he read it:

> When you were enlightened, Jun-zōsu (Ikkyū), I
> gave you a paper of Buddhist words. You asked me
> why I wanted a stake to tie the ass to, and went off,
> dusting your sleeves.... When the True Law of
> Rinzai is lost, you must bring it back again. You
> are my child; keep this in your heart; think of it.
>
> May, the 27th Year of Oei,
> Kasō

Ikkyū's life from now on was spent in teaching the
people, and condemning the sham monks of his (and
all) time, but whether he lived alone in a poor hut
or in Daitokuji Temple, he was surrounded by zealous
disciples. In 1467 civil war broke out, Kyōto was
devastated, and Ikkyū spent a wandering life in Yamato,
Izumi, and Settsu. In 1475, Ikkyū was asked by the
Emperor to become the head of Daitokuji Temple. He
was unable to refuse this position of great honour, but
expressed his feelings in the following verse:

> The disciples of Daitokuji have extinguished the
>   guttering lamp;
> It is difficult for them to understand the poetical
>   feeling of an icy night;
> For fifty years I was a man wearing straw rain-
>   coat and umbrella-hat;
> I feel grief and shame now at this purple robe.

The same year he rebuilt the Hall of the Law which had been lost by fire during the civil war, and two years after, the Great Gate and other gates were reconstructed. This winter he fell ill and died suddenly on the 21st of November 1481 at the age of eighty eight. His death poem is said to be the following:

> Dimly, for thirty years;
> Faintly for thirty years,—
> Dimly and faintly for sixty years:
> At my death, I pass my faeces and offer them to
> Brahma.

On a portrait of himself, Ikkyū has written:

> The willow is green, the flower red;
> The pilgrimage is over.
> Today, at this season,
> I break my staff,
> And burn it in the snows of July.

But on another occasion he says the same thing in a very different way:

> Life, death? Death, life?
> The willow is green, the flower is red.
> Kwatz !
> The willow is not green, the flower is not red;
> Beware ! beware !

Ikkyū is warning us not to fall into science or fantasy, into unity or diversity, into fact or paradox.

Coming to the works of Ikkyū, there is unfortunately and oddly no collection of his sayings. We have instead a very doubtful collection of humorous stories in *Ikkyū-Banashi*, 1700, and *Zoku Ikkyū-Banashi*, 1725. Like Ōka Tadasuke, 1677-1751, who had a great reputation as a shrewd lawyer, and about whom so many anecdotes have collected, Ikkyū was so vivaciously and profoundly witty that stories of his doings and sayings have increased like a rolling snowball, and it is impossible at this time, five hundred years afterwards, to distinguish the true from the false anecdotes. We have the *Kyōunshū*, three volumes of Chinese poetry. These

consist of the versifying of old kōans; poems deploring
the conditions of his time; and verses expressing his
experience of life. They may be compared to the
similar verses of the Chinese hermit and eccentric,
Hanzan. An example:

Raindropping

This sobbing without the door,—what voice is this?
Should you not know, the one to go and ask is Kyōsei.
Ordinary people are upside down, and deludedly
running after things;
Before my window, at midnight, the lamp burns blue.

The first three lines are practically a transcription of
the 46th Case of *Hekiganroku,* where the meaning is
that it is not difficult to hear the sound of the rain as
the Voice of God, but far from easy to come back from
this to a realm where illusion and enlightenment are
(seen as) the same thing. This is what is meant perhaps
by the last line of the poem. Kyōsei succeeded Seppō,
822-908, a famous Chinese Zen master.

Gaikotsu, The Skeleton, which has illustrations and
waka inserted in it, speaks of death and the transitori-
ness of the world in a rather Shinshū-like way. *Bukki-
gun,* The Bodhisattva and Demon Armies, is the story
of how Amida and Kannon lead a sort of Salvation
Army against Hell, but together with Dainichi Nyorai
they make Hell, as it is, Paradise. In *Futari Bikuni,*
The Two Nuns, one nun visits another and asks her
about Buddhism. There is in it an interesting waka
concerning the religious mind, the blossoming heart:

If you break open
The cherry tree,
Where are the flowers?
But in springtime,
See how they bloom!

Kanahōgo, An Easy Sermon, gives us Ikkyū's rather
pessimistic view of life, arising partly from his own
double character, both mirthful and melancholy, and

from the depressing social and religious conditions of his times. Perhaps the commonest word, one that represents the spirit of that age, and the Japanese world-view of any age, is "dream." Ikkyū quotes a waka of Musō Kokushi, 1271-1346, composed when he was enlightened:

> Born like a dream
> In this dream of a world,
>   How easy in mind I am,
> I who will fade away
> Like the morning dew.

Mizukagami, The Water Mirror, is an easy discourse on Buddhism with waka and kyōka (mad poems) mixed, and with notes by Mori Daikyō. One of the verses:

> The mind,—
> But if there is really
>   No such thing as the mind,
> With what enlightenment
> Shall it be enlightened?

Satori is to know that there is no such thing as *satori.*

Amida-hadaka-monogatari, Naked Speaking about Amida, is Ikkyū's answer to a man who asked him if Amida's Paradise in the West really exists. Ikkyū replies to the effect that the teaching of the Pure Land Sect and the Zen Sect are really the same in essence, and quotes an old waka:

> Vainly
> Seeking Amida
>   In the West,
> Not knowing
> He is in the South.

There is here an untranslatable pun on *minami,* south, and *minna mi,* all in the body, that is, inside one's own body. Amida is in the soul or nowhere, but if the Kingdom of Heaven is not within us, we say it is in the sky or in the West. There is also a commentary by Ikkyū on the *Prajnaparamita-Hridaya Sutra*

(*Hannyashin-gyō*) the shortest of all the sutras, only
one page in the original or translations; it expresses
in abstract contradictions the transcendentalism of Zen.
Ikkyū's commentary is very "kind," being in fact rather
Buddhistic than Zen, and becomes tedious, with him
explaining like a Sunday School teacher the Six Dusts,
the Twelve Links in the Chain of Existence, and so on.
Two Nō plays, *Eguchi* and *Yamauba* have been attributed to him. About a hundred and fifty *dōka* or
Buddhist waka remain, most of them very good.

Ikkyū's life and character are full of contradictions.
He is a Buddhist priest, obeying all the Buddhist rules;
but he is also a Zen priest, breaking any law freely.
He was a son of the Emperor; but lived in the direst
poverty for many years. He had very great political
influence; and yet he was not given any office until
made head of Daitokuji Temple in his eighty-first year.
He was an enlightened man in the true and religious
sense; nevertheless he twice attempted suicide, once
in his youth, once in his old age. He has more contradictions in him than Hamlet, and yet, he is, in the
words of Hazlitt, "always, amid every fluctuation of
feeling, every shifting of intelligence, one and the same
man of genius."

IKKYU'S DŌKA

"Dōka" are didactic waka, moralizing, and usually Buddhistic, seldom if ever of great poetical value, and usually of easy popular comprehension. Ikkyū wrote about a hundred and fifty of these poems, many of which are well known. Eighty of the best are given here. Ikkyū's dōka, unlike his Chinese poems, often give us the ancient melancholy of primitive Buddhism, the same feeling that life is suffering which we find in the *Hōjōki* and the *Sarashina Diary*. But many others are full of the contradictions of Zen, yet portray for us a man of deep sincerity, too honest perhaps to be a great lyrical poet.

1. 有漏ぢより無漏ぢへかへる一やすみ
     あめふらばふれ風ふかばふけ

Uroji yori muroji e kaeru hito yasumi
Ame furaba fure kaze fukaba fuke

A rest on the way back
From the Leaky Road
To the Never-leaking Road;
If it rains, let it rain;
If it blows, let it blow.

The Leaky Road is this world, the Never-leaking Road the world before we (and it) were born. The "way back" is the return to ante-natal existence. The "rest" is our short human life, so short that rain or wind, grief or passion, are of little moment or meaning. The *hito yasumi*, "one rest," is Ikkyū's own name, whose meaning he seems to be explaining in this verse.

2. 本らいもなきいにしへの我なれば
     死ゆくかたも何もかもなし

Honrai mo naki inishie no ware nareba
Shini yuku kata mo nani mo ka mo nashi

My self of long ago,
    In nature non-existent;
Nowhere to go when dead,
    Nothing at all.

Before birth we were non-existent, and we shall be so after death. We are therefore in this condition at the present moment, *mu-ichi-motsu,* without a thing in the world we can call our own.

3. 問へばいふとはねばいはぬ達磨どの
    こゝろのうちになにかあるべき

Toeba iu towaneba iwanu daruma dono
Kokoro no uchi ni nani ka aru beki

When asked, he answered;
    No question, no answer;
        Then Master Daruma
Must have had
Nothing in his mind.

When the mind is like a mirror, undistorted by passion and unclouded by thought, everything appears as it is, and there is no hallucination. Daruma answered when he was questioned, said nothing when not questioned, ate when he was hungry, slept when he was tired. This is the true life of a human being.

4. はじめなくをはりもなきにわがこゝろ
    うまれ死するも空の空なり

Hajime naku owari mo naki ni waga kokoro
Umare shisuru mo kū no kū nari

Our mind,—
    Without end,
        Without beginning,
Though it is born, though it dies,—
The essence of emptiness!

This is what Sir Thomas Browne at the end of *Hydriotaphia* calls: "Ready to be anything, in the ecstasy of being ever." By "to be anything" he means the timeless life.

5.　三とせまでつくりしつみももろともに
　　　つひにはわれもきえはてにけり

Mitose made tsukurishi tsumi mo morotomo ni
Tsui ni wa ware mo kiehate ni keri

> All the sins committed
> 　　In the Three Worlds
> Will fade and disappear
> 　　Together with myself.

"The Three Worlds" are the past, present, and future. If there is no good, there is no bad. If there is no sinner, there is no sin. What we call "our" life belongs to the universe, and what we call our good and bad deeds also.

6.　ゆくすえにやどをそことも定めねば
　　　ふみまよふべきみちもなきかな

Yukusue ni yado wo soko tomo sadameneba
Fumi mayou beki michi mo naki kana

> If at the end of our journey
> 　　There be no final resting place,
> How can there be
> 　　A way to lose ourselves in?

There lies concealed in this verse the paradox that when we realize that our sins are not real, we cease to do those very things which appeared to be sins.

7.　釈迦といふいたづらものが世にいでて
　　　おほくの人をまよはするかな

Shaka to iu itazura mono ga yo ni idete
Ōku no hito wo mayowasuru kana

> Shakamuni,
> That mischievous creature,
> 　　Having appeared in the world,
> Misled, alas,
> How many people!

This verse is a personal expression of the previous verse. If we think our sins are real sins, if we think evil is an actual and positive thing, we can never get rid of it. If there is a "Way" as Shakamuni taught, there must be illusion,—but the great illusion is to think that there is illusion.,

8. 心とはいかなるものをいふやらん
   すみ絵にかきし松風の音

   Kokoro towa ikanaru mono wo iu yaran
   Sumie ni kakishi matsukaze no oto

   > The mind,—
   > What shall we call it?
   > It is the sound of the breeze
   > That blows through the pines
   > In the Indian-ink picture.

There are other phrases which express the nature of the mind, for example, the sound of one hand clapped, the sound of the voice of a crow that does not crow on a dark night, a man's shape before he is born. All these are to convey the idea that the mind is not something, though it is not nothing, for after all, we do see and feel something in the picture of the pine trees.

9. そのまゝにうまれながらの心こそ
   ねかはすとても仏なるべし

   Sono mama ni umare nagara no kokoro koso
   Negawazu totemo hotoke naru beshi

   > The mind remaining
   > Just as it was born,—
   > Without any prayer
   > It becomes the Buddha.

This verse expresses in gently poetic words what is coldly and philosophically stated as: All men have the Buddha nature.

10. 嘘をつきぢごくへおつるものならば
    なきことつくるしゃかいかにせん

    Uso wo tsuki jigoku e otsuru mono naraba
    Naki koto tsukuru shaka ikani sen

    > Tell a lie,
    > And you fall into Hell.
    > Then what will happen to Buddha
    > Who contrived
    > Things that don't exist?

This verse does not mean that, as the saying is, *uso mo hōben,* "Lies also are means (to a good end)," but that all teaching, the teaching of the Buddha included, is false in so far as it expresses in words that truth which can never be expressed in words. The Buddha tells us the way of salvation,—but there is no way, no salvation. All men are saved just as they are; the way is the very path that you tread under your feet at this moment,—but this that I write also is all lies and nonsense.

11.　　つくりをく罪の須弥ほどあるならば
　　　　えんまの帳につけどころなし

　　Tsukuri oku tsumi no shumi hodo aru naraba
　　Emma no chō ni tsukedokoro nashi

> If the sins we commit
> 　Are as great as Mt. Sumeru,
> There will be no room for them
> 　In the records of Emma.

Put into a Christian form, "If we commit an infinite number of unforgivable sins, there is the infinite love of Christ which will pardon and annul them all."

12.　　極楽もぢごくもしらぬ思ひでに
　　　　うまれぬさきのものとなるべし

　　Gokuraku mo jigoku mo shiranu omoide ni
　　Umarenu saki no mono to narubeshi

> Of Heaven or Hell we have
> 　No recollection, no knowledge;
> We must become what we were
> 　Before we were born.

If there is Heaven or Hell for us after death, there must have been Heaven or Hell for us before birth. But we have no recollection of such a condition. Therefore all we can say is that into that state we came from, we go once more.

13.　　雨あられ雪や氷とへだつれど
　　　　おつればおなじ谷川の水

Ame arare yuki ya kōri to hedatsuredo
  Otsureba onaji tanigawa no mizu

> Rain, hail, snow and ice
> Are divided from one another;
> But after they fall,
> They are the same water
> Of the stream in the valley.

Rain, hail, snow and ice are different forms of the same thing; so with enlightenment and illusion, goodness and badness, beauty and ugliness, truth and error. To know this in the head is to have knowledge; to know it in the body is to have wisdom.

14.　夜もすがら仏の道をたづねれば
　　　わがこゝろにぞたづねいりける

Yomosugara hotoke no michi wo tazunereba
Waga kokoro ni zo tazune iri keru

> Should you seek
> The way of the Buddha
> All night long,
> Searching, you will enter
> Into your own mind.

We feel that the Truth must be somewhere outside us, since inside ourselves we find nothing but confusion, camouflage, and concupiscence. But in books, in others, in the whole wide universe no God is to be found. God is that very intellectual chaos, hypocrisy and physical passion which we deplore.

15.　国いづくさとはいかにと人とはゞ
　　　本来無為のものとこたへよ

Kuni izuku sato wa ikani to hito towaba
Honrai mui no mono to kotae yo

> When they ask you,
> "Where is your country?
> 　What is your native place?" answer,
> "I am a man
> Of Original Inactivity."

We come from nothing and go to nothing. This "nothing," which is not nothingness, is our real home.

16.　本来の面目坊が立姿
　　　ひとめ見しより恋とこそなれ

Honrai no membokubō ga tachisugata
Hitome mishi yori koi to kose nare

The figure of the Real Man
　Standing there,—
Just a glimpse of him,
　And we are in love.

Home again. But what was home? The fish has
the vast ocean for home. And man has timelessness
and nowhere. "I won't delude myself with the
fallacy of home," he said to himself. "The four walls
are a blanket I wrap around in, in timelessness and
nowhere, to go to sleep." (*Kangaroo*).

Blake says in the *Proverbs of Hell*, "Truth can never
be told so as to be understood, and not be believ'd."
Every scrap of goodness or truth or beauty, and at
the same time all badness, error and ugliness are, as
Dante says,

　Naught but a vestige of the Light,
　Half-understood, which shines through that thing.

17.　ふらばふれふらずばふらずふらずとも
　　　ぬれてゆくべき袖ならばこそ

Furaba fure furazuba furazu furazu tomo
Nurete yuku beki sode naraba koso

　　If it rain, let it rain;
　If it rain not, let it not rain;
　　But even should it not rain,
　You must travel
　With wet sleeves.

What must happen, of good or ill, must happen. But
even if our lives should have but comparatively little
disaster and sorrow, the end of it is old age and death
for ourselves and those we love.

18.　花を見よ色香もともにちりはてゝ
　　　こゝろなくても春は来にけり

Hana wo mi yo iroka mo tomo ni chiri hatete
Kokoro nakute mo haru wa ki ni keri

> Look at the cherry blossoms!
> Their colour and scent fall with them,
>> Are gone for ever,
> Yet mindless
> The spring comes again.

Here again we have the same lesson. When the flowers fall, scent and hue disappear with them, but the next spring some unseen, unthinking, unthought power makes them bloom again with the same perfume and colour. Emily Brontë says:

> Strange power, I trust thy might;
> Trust thou my constancy.

19.　へつらひてたのしきよりもへつらはで
　　　まづしき身こそこゝろやすけれ

Hetsuraite tanoshiki yori mo hetsurawade
Mazushiki mi koso kokoro yasukere

> Better than flattering
>> And living pleasantly,
> Is not to flatter,
>> And rest at ease in poverty.

Perhaps Ikkyū was thinking of Tōenmei, 365-427 A.D., one of the most famous of those who would not "bend their backs" to obtain office of fame.

20.　仏法はなべのさかやき石の髭
　　　絵にかく竹のともずれの声

Buppo wa nabe no sakayaki ishi no hige
E ni kaku take no tomozure no koe

> Buddhism
> Is the shaved part of the saucepan,
>> The whiskers of the pebble,
> The sound that accompanies
> The bamboos in the picture.

From the Buddhist point of view, the whiskers of the saucepan and the pebble are not non-existent things. This we see faintly adumbrated in the sound of the bamboos in the picture. Whiskers are latent in the pebble, just as the flower is hidden in the root of the tree. Thus Buddhism is not a thing, not a law, not a principle even, yet it far indeed from nothing at all.

21.　傀儡師首にかけたる人形箱
　　　　鬼をださふと仏ださふと

Kairaishi kubi ni kaketaru ningyo-bako
Oni wo dasō to hotoke dasō to

> The puppet-player hangs them
> Round his neck, not his heart;
> He can take out a Devil,
> He can take out a Buddha.

An even better illustration would be that of a conjurer, who takes out of a perfectly empty box all kinds of strange things. The mind, the heart, is so. It is void and vacant, yet from this nothing we create the world. This god-like power is possessed by everyone, but best seen in such people as Shakespeare or Dickens.

22.　べちのことなきぞといふもはやそむく
　　　　つひにいひえぬだるま一休

Bechi no koto naki zo to iū mo haya somuku
Tsui ni iienu Daruma Ikkyū

> If he says,
> "There is nothing special about it,"
> Already he has transgressed,
> And can say nothing else,
> This Daruma Ikkyū.

If we say the teaching of Buddhism is the truth, this is wrong. But if we say, "This is wrong; there is nothing special about the teaching of Buddha," this also is wrong and equally wrong. Whatever we say, it is wrong.

23.　わが宿ははしらもたてずふきもせず
　　　　雨にもぬれず風もあたらず

Waga yado wa hashira mo tatezu fuki mo sezu
Ame ni mo nurezu kaze mo atarazu

> My abiding place
> Has no pillars;

> It is roofless,—
>   Yet the rain does not wet it,
> Nor the wind strike it.

If we have a house, the roof will leak. If we live by some principle, there will be troublesome exceptions. If we take the rain as it comes, we shall never get wet.

24.   ふくときはうべさわがしき山風も
　　　ふかぬときにはふかぬなりけり

Fuku toki wa ube sawagashiki yamakaze mo
Fukanu toki ni wa fukanu nari keri

> When it blows,
>   The mountain wind is boisterous,
> But when it blows not,
>   It simply blows not.

When the wind blows, it blows mindlessly; when it does not blow, it is mindlessly calm. Nothing comes into existence or goes out of existence. Things *simply* happen or *simply* do not happen.

25.   はしなくて雲のそらへはあがるとも
　　　くどんの経をたのまれやせん

Hashi nakute kumo no sora e wa agaru tomo
Kudon no kyō wo tanomare ya sen

> Though it has no bridge,
>   The cloud climbs up to heaven;
> It does not ask aid
>   Of Gautama's sutras.

Kudon is the transliterated form of Gautama. We, like the clouds, may climb to heaven by our own lightness, without asking the help of any words of wisdom.

26.   ほらぬ井にたまらぬ水の浪たちて
　　　かげもかたちもなき人ぞくむ

Horanu i ni tamaranu mizu no nami tachite
Kage mo katachi mo naki hito zo kumu

> Ripples appear
> On the unaccumulated water

Of the undug well,
As the formless, bodiless man
Draws water from it.

This verse points to the other side of the double-
faced world of which we commonly see only one side.
There is a well, but at the same time it is undug. Here
is a man riding with two others, but he is dead already:

So the two brothers with their murdered man
Rode on toward fair Florence.

We must never forget the whole world, of which
the dichotomous intellect shows us either the here or
the there, either the then or the now.

27.   心とてげにもこゝろはなきものを
          さとりはなにのさとりなるらん

*Kokoro tote ge ni mo kokoro wa naki mono wo
Satori wa nani no satori naruran*

The mind:
Since there is really
No such thing as mind,
With what enlightenment,—
Shall it be enlightened?

Enlightenment means knowing that there is no illusion, that is, it means knowing that there is no such
thing as enlightenment.

28.   みな人のねはん常楽しらすして
          生死無常をなげくあはれさ

*Mina hito no nehan jōraku shirazu shite
Shōji mujō wo nageku aware sa*

Pitiful are
People who do not know
Nirvana and its eternal felicity!
How they grieve
At life, death, and mutability!

In our deepest nature, we are unborn, undying; but
we do not know or forget this, and our life is one long
endeavour to escape from the inevitable, to remain
changeless in a world of change.

29. 釈迦も又あみだももとは人ぞかし
   われもかたちは人にあらすや

Shaka mo mata Amida mo moto wa hito zo kashi
Ware mo katachi wa hito ni arazu ya

> Shaka, and Amida too,
> > Were originally human beings;
> Have I not also
> > The form of a man?

We see in the verse a rather deep difference between Christianity and Buddhism. According to the former, we are sons of God. According to the latter, we are God, not a part of God, not a slice of the cake, but the whole cake.

30. 妙なりし法のはちすの花の身は
   幾世ふるとも色はかはらじ

Tae narishi nori no hachisu no hana no mi wa
Ikuyo furu tomo iro wa kawaraji

> Wonderful, indeed,
> > The Lotus Flower of the Law!
> However many ages may pass,
> > Still that same colour.

The unchanging colour of the flower of the lotus is (not a symbol, but the very same thing) our Buddha nature which Pope describes with eighteenth century formality and abstraction:

> As perfect is in hair as heart.

31. 三日月のみつれはかけて跡もなし
   とにかくにまたあり明の月

Mikazuki no mitsureba kakete ato mo nashi
Tonikaku ni mata ariake no tsuki

> The crescent moon
> Becomes full, and wanes,
> > And nothing is left;
> But still, there in the dawn,
> > The crescent moon!

Just as the moon disappears, but does not cease to exist, so individual life ceases, but the general life,

the life of nature persists. So, individually also, there
is birth, life, and death, but our eternal, that is, our
timeless life never ends, because it is beyond the power
of time.

32.　　見るごとにみなそのまゝのすがたかな
　　　　　柳はみどり花はくれない

    Miru goto ni mina sono mama no sugata kana
    Yanagi wa midori hana wa kurenai

> Whenever we see them, all are
> Just as they are:
> The willow is green,
> The flower is red.

The willow is green. But in reality, we say, it is
colourless. This is so. But at the same time, it is green.
When we know it has no colour, then for the first
time we see how deeply green it is.

33.　　たびはたゞうきものなるにふる里の
　　　　　そらにかへるをいとふはかなさ

    Tabi wa tada uki mono naru ni furusato no
    Sora ni kaeru wo itou hakanasa

> Since the journey of life
> Is little but grief and pain,
> Why should we be so reluctant
> To return to the sky of our native place?

Our "native place" is the state we were in before
birth. Ikkyū seems to mean that usually when on a
journey we enjoy ourselves and are unwilling to
return home, but our journey through this world is
so full of wants and woes that it is strange that we
should not wish to return to our pre-natal condition,
"to God who is our home."

34.　　かきおくも夢のうちなるしるしかな
　　　　　さめてはさらにとふ人もなし

    Kakioku mo yume no uchi naru shirushi kana
    Samete wa sara ni tou hito mo nashi

> To write something and leave it behind us,
> It is but a dream.

When we awake we know
    There is not even anyone to read it.

This verse is the conclusion of *The Skeleton*. It is
in this transcendental spirit that Shakespeare wrote
his plays, careless, so it seems, whether after all that
labour and ecstasy they should survive in the form he
wrote them, careless even whether they should survive
at all.

35.　　我が法をいはでもいらぬ春の花も
　　　　ひらけてちりてつちとこそなれ

*Waga hō wo iwade mo iranu haru no hana mo
Hirakete chirite tsuchi to koso nare*

Though we do not preach the doctrine,
    Unasked the flowers bloom in spring;
They fall and scatter,
    They turn to dust.

After all, what is the Law, the Doctrine? Only that
flowers bloom and fade. There is one thing more, however, to do, what Ikkyū has done here, express this
fact in our art, in our lives.

36.　　をのれさへ熱気はらはぬ不動めが
　　　　悪魔降服無用なりけり

*Onore sae nekki harawanu fudō-me ga
Akuma kōfuku muyō nari keri*

How on earth could that chap Fudō,
    Who cannot drive his own heat away,
    Make the Evil spirits submit?

They said, quite rightly, of Christ, "He saved others,
himself he cannot save," the implication of the irony
being that if he could not save himself, how could he
save others? Fudō (here taken as the God of Fire)
cannot extinguish his own fire, much less that of others;
anger cannot drive out anger. This is the teaching of
the Hokkukyō, the Dhammapada.

37.　　門松はめいどのたびの一里づか
　　　　馬かごもなくとまりやもなし

Kadomatsu wa meido no tabi no ichirizuka
Uma kago mo naku tomariya mo nashi

> The New Year Pine Decorations
> Are a milestone on the journey
> To the other world;
> There is no horse, no palanquin,
> No lodging-house.

What we ordinarily and stupidly think of as some-thing congratulatory is really a matter for condolence. We are one step nearer the grave. And there is no need of "transportation" for this short journey of ours; the mere passage of time is enough.

38.　生れては死ぬるなりけりおしなべて
　　　しゃかもだるまもねこも杓子も

Umarete wa shinuru nari keri oshinabete
Shaka mo daruma mo neko mo shakushi mo

> We are born, we die.
> All are the same,
> Shakamuni, Daruma,
> The cat and the ladle.

This is the real democracy, the democracy of nature, the democracy of death.

39.　ほとけにもなりかたまるはいらぬもの
　　　石仏らを見るにつけても

Hotoke ni mo nari katamaru wa iranu mono
Ishibotoke ra wo miru ni tsukete mo

> To harden into a Buddha is wrong;
> All the more I think so
> When I look at a stone Buddha.

It is the nature of man, (that is to say his biological nature,) to harden into something or other. Eternal life means having it without hardening, having it abundantly and overflowingly.

40.　ひとり来てひとりかへるも迷なり
　　　きたらず去らぬ道ををしへん

Hitori kite hitori kaeru mo mayoi nari
Kitarazu saranu michi wo oshien

"We come into this world alone,
We depart alone",—
    This also is illusion.
I will teach you the way
Not to come, not to go!

Ikkyū wishes us to live always in the spaceless, timeless world, where there is no birth and death, no coming and going, for these are unknown in the universe as a whole.

41.　世の中はくふてはこしてねて起きて
　　　さてそのあとは死ぬるばかりぞ

Yo no naka wa kūte hakoshite nete okite
Sate sono ato wa shinuru bakari zo

We eat, excrete, sleep, and get up;
    This is our world.
All we have to do after that,—
    Is to die.

The *Rubaiyat* says, almost as laconically:

Some little talk awhile of Me and Thee
There was—and then no more of Thee and Me.

42.　死にはせぬどこへも行かぬこゝに居る
　　　たづねはするなものは言はぬぞ

Shini wa senu doko e mo yukanu koko ni iru
Tazune wa suruna mono wa iwanu zo

I shan't die, I shan't go anywhere,
    I'll be here;
But don't ask me anything,
    I shan't answer.

This is said to be Ikkyū's death verse, but whether so or not it is very good, expressing as it does, so concretely and simply, the contradictions that make up our life and death.

43.　なにごともみな偽の世なりけり
　　　しぬるといふもまことならねば

Nanigoto mo mina itsuwari no yo nari keri
Shinuru to iu mo makoto naraneba

Whatsoever it may be,
     It is all part of the world of illusion,
Death itself
     Not being a real thing.

This verse comes in *Two Nuns,* in answer to the
question, "What happens when people die?" Ikkyū
calls the above verse "the medicine of Unborn-
Undying." If death is not something real, why should
we fear it? And what else is there to fear? "Death
once dead, there's no more dying then."

44.　道はたゞせけん世外のこと〵もに
　　　　じひしんじつの人にたづねよ

　　Michi wa tada seken segai no koto tomo ni
　　Jihi shinjitsu no hito ni tazuneyo

Should you wish to know the way
     In both this world,
And that other,
     Ask a man of mercy and sincerity.

The eye of the artist and the eye of the scientist see
harmony. The religious, the moral eye sees disharmony; it views with horror the universal cat eating
the universal rat. Ikkyū says here that after all the
merciful (not sentimental) eye is the ultimate standard.

45.　妙にして神あるものは心かな
　　　　天地にわたりみじんにも入る

　　Tae ni shite kami aru mono wa kokoro kana
　　Tenchi ni watari mijin ni mo iru

How marvellous,
     How god-like the mind of man!
It fills the whole universe!
     It enters every mote of dust!

Emerson says:

     There is no great and no small
     To the soul that maketh all,
     But where it goes all things are,
     And it goeth everywhere.

There is here something also akin to Blake in his, "Truth is in minute particulars," and "One thought fills Immensity."

46.　なにことも人の心にさかふこそ
　　　世法仏法さはりなりけり

> *Nanigoto mo hito no kokoro ni sakau koso*
> *Sehō Buppō sawari nari keri*

> Whatever runs counter
>   To the mind and will of ordinary people
> Hinders the Law of Men
>   And the Law of Buddha.

Whitman says, "Only what nobody denies is true," and Ikkyū also feels here the truth of human nature, for this nature is after all the Buddha nature. Vox populi, vox dei.

47.　なにをがなまいらせたくとおもへども
　　　達磨宗には一物もなし

> *Nani wo gana mairasetaku to omoe domo*
> *Darumashū ni wa ichimotsu mo nashi*

> I would like
>   To offer you something,
> But in the Daruma Sect
>   We have nothing at all.

This verse, so witty, so true, is one of Ikkyū's best. It might be used at a feast, or at a funeral.

48.　山城のうりやなすびをそのまゝに
　　　たむけとなれや賀茂川の水

> *Yamashiro no uri ya nasubi wo sono mama ni*
> *Tamuke to nare ya kamogawa no mizu*

> All the melons and egg-plants
> Of Yamashiro, just as they are,
>   And all the waters of the River Kamo,
> Shall be the offerings
>   At the Feast of All Souls.

This verse expresses Ikkyū's feeling that it is not our individual puny offerings to the Buddha that are of importance, but rather the feeling that "All the Earth is the Lord's and the fullness thereof."

49.　一休が身をば身ほどに思わねば
　　　市も山家も同じ住家よ

Ikkyū ga mi wo ba mi hodo ni omowaneba
Ichi mo yamaga mo onaji sumika yo

> As Ikkyū does not think of his body
> As if it were his body,
> He lives in the same place,
> Whether it is town or country.

It is a mistake to live in solitude, whether it is a city or a mountain recess. We are alone with our closest friend; even Robinson Crusoe was not alone on his island.

50.　音もなく香もなき人の心にて
　　　よべばこたふるぬしもぬすびと

Oto mo naku ka mo naki hito no kokoro nite
Yobeba kotauru nushi mo nusubito

> The mind of man is without sound,
> Without odour;
> He who answers when called
> Is nothing but a thief.

The real nature of man has no smell, no sound, no taste; it is invisible and untouchable. How then can we reply when someone speaks to us, without borrowing, or stealing as Ikkyū says, words that do not belong to us? How can words in any way represent the soul, of which they are no part whatever?

51.　ありと言へばありとや人のおもふらん
　　　こたへてもなき山彦の声

Ari to ieba ari to ya hitono omouran
Kotaete mo naki yamabiko no koe

> If we say "There is,"
> People think "There is";
> But though it answers,
> It is not,
> This mountain echo.

When we say that the mountain echo exists, people think there is something there. But when we go to the mountain, however much we call up hill and down dale, no echo can we discover.

52. なしといへばなしとや人のおもふらん
　　　こたへもぞする山彦の声

Nashi to ieba nashi to ya hito no omouran
Kotae mo zo suru yamabiko no koe

> If we say, "There is not,"
> 　　People think "There is not,"
> Though it answers,
> 　　The mountain echo.

When we say that every thing is "empty of self-nature," people think that there is really nothing at all. An echo is something non-existent, yet it is always "there," ready to answer to our calling.

53. ゆく水にかずかくよりもはかなきは
　　　仏をたのむ人ののちの世

Yuku mizu ni kazu kaku yori mo hakanaki wa
Hotoke wo tanomu hito no nochi no yo

> More frail and illusory
> 　　Than numbers written on water,
> Our seeking from the Buddha
> 　　Felicity in the after-world.

To ask the Buddha to help us, in time, is foolish for two reasons. First, because he will not do so. Second, because we are by nature unborn, undying, timeless, eternal, omnipotent.

54. いまははやこゝろにかゝる雲もなし
　　　月のいるべき山しなければ

Ima wa haya kokoro ni kakaru kumo mo nashi
Tsuki no irubeki yama shi nakereba

> Already, over the heart
> 　　Not a cloud is hanging,
> And no mountain is there
> 　　For the moon to hide behind.

This verse expresses, with a singular elation, that "serene and blessed mood" in which all painful and pleasant things are seen as good and necessary. Wordsworth says the same thing in *Tintern Abbey*, though in different words:

All that we behold is full of blessings.

55.   世の中の生死の道につれはなし
　　　たゞさびしくも独死独来

Yo no naka no Shōshi no michi ni tsure wa nashi
Tada sabishiku mo doku-shi doku-rai

> In our way through this world
> Of birth and death,
> 　　We have no companion;
> Lonely we die,
> Alone we are born.

This verse has more of Buddhism than of Zen in it, more of weakness than of strength, but all the more, perhaps, of human nature. The death that we fear, that we grieve for, is not so much for ourselves, as the separation from those with whom we are united by some secret tie, unbreakable by time. So Emerson says, in *Threnody*:

> The eager fate which carried thee
> Took the largest part of me;
> For this losing is true dying;
> This is lordly man's down-lying,
> This his slow but sure reclining,
> Star by star his world resigning.

56.   大水のさきにながるゝとちがらも
　　　身をすてゝこそ浮かぶせもあれ

Ōmizu no saki ni nagaruru tochigara mo
Mi wo sutete koso ukabu se mo are

> The vast flood
> 　　Rolls onward
> But yield yourself,
> 　　And it floats you upon it.

When we realize that we do not live, but *are lived* by some "power, not ourselves, that makes for righteousness," we float down the stream of time never submerged, because we always do what Stevenson tells us to do, "travel light." Wordsworth says:

I made no vows, but vows were made for me.

57.　なにごとも見ざるいわざるきかざるは
　　　たゞほとけにもまさるなりけり

Nanigoto mo mizaru iwazaru kikazaru wa
Tada hotoke nimo masaru narikeri

> Who sees naught,
> Says naught,
> Hears naught,
> Simply surpasses
> The Buddha.

To speak as not speaking, to hear as if we had not heard, this is to live in Nirvana while still in this world. To walk as if not walking, to do a kindness as though conferring no favour,—this is living truly.

58.　有無をのする生死の海のあま小舟
　　　底ぬけて後有無もたまらず

Umu wo nosuru seishi no umi no ama obune
Soko nukete nochi umu mo tamarazu

> On the sea of death and life,
> The diver's boat is freighted
> With "Is" and "Is not";
> But if the bottom is broken through,
> "Is" and "Is not" disappear.

To get rid of the relativity of the outer world is impossible. What we can do is to break through the bottom of our own desiring and loathing.

59.　口ほどに身の行ひのならざれば
　　　わが心にもはぢられぞする

Kuchi hodo ni mi no okonai no narazareba
Waga kokoro nimo hajirare zo suru

> What my body does, accords not
> With what my mouth utters,

> And my heart
> Is full of shame.

Since there is no man living or dead who could not say this, the only thing for us all to do is to talk less.

60. 仏には心もならず身もならず
    ならぬものこそ仏なりけり

Hotoke niwa kokoro mo narazu mi mo narazu
Naranu mono koso hotoke narikeri

> The mind cannot become the Buddha;
>   The body cannot become the Buddha;
> Only what cannot become the Buddha
>   Can become the Buddha.

Ikkyū asserts here the unqualifyability, the indefinability, and yet the reality of the Buddha.

61. 奥山にむすばずとても柴の庵
    こゝろからにて世をいとふべし

Okuyama ni musubazu totemo shiba no io
Kokoro kara nite yo wo itou beshi

> I don't build myself
> A grass-roofed hut
>   In the deepest mountains,
> Nevertheless, I loathe
> This world.

To hate money and possessions and power and fame, it is not necessary to avoid men or live outside society. Indeed, to do so often results in a hankering after the very things we pretend to despise.

62. 露ときえまぼろしと覚ふいなづまの
    かげのごとくに身は思ふべし

Tsuyu to kie maboroshi to obou inazuma no
Kage no gotoku ni mi wa omou beshi

> As lightning
>   Which disappears like dew,
> Which vanishes like a phantom,—
>   Thus think of yourself.

To the extent that we know that all is a phantom, of no self-nature, to that extent we will be unattached to things, to life itself. Then anger, though it does not disappear, becomes more impersonal. The fear of death, though ever-present, is allayed. Our own eternal fate, the existence of God, the final outcome of all things,—these lose their oppressive importance.

63.　仏とてほかにもとむるこゝろこそ
　　　まよひの中のまよひなりける

Hotoke tote hoka ni motomuru kokoro koso
Mayoi no naka no mayoi nari keru

> A mind to search elsewhere
> 　　For the Buddha,
> Is the foolishness
> 　　In the very centre of foolishness.

Our mistake is to look for truth outside, or inside ourselves. The great mistake is to look at all, for what we always were, and always will be, is not to be found or attained. In some supremely odd way, we are the Buddha, and this place is the Earthly Paradise.

64.　はちす葉のにごりにそまぬ露の身は
　　　たゞそのまゝに真如実相

Hachisu-ba no nigori ni somanu tsuyu no mi wa
Tada sono mama ni shinnyo jissō

> The dew on the lotus leaf
> 　　Undyed by its colour,
> Just as it is,
> 　　Is the Real Form of Buddha.

We are like the dew, seemingly frail and fleeting, but really timeless; undyed by circumstance, untainted by sin, undiminished by death. We, just as we are, are the Real Form of Buddha.

65.　物ごとに執着せざる心こそ
　　　無想無心の無住なりけり

Monogoto ni shūjaku sezaru kokoro koso
Musō mushin no mujū nari keri

The mind which is unattached
  To all things in the world,
Does not think, does not feel,
  Is fluid and flexible.

We are to look at the fleeting ephemeral scenes of
this world with a mind that is equally fleeting and
ephemeral. Then the seer and the seen are one; the
seeing is a property of both.

66.   一切の諸仏菩薩も悲願より
          ぼだいねはんは成就し玉ふ。

> *Issai no shobutsu bosatsu mo higan yori*
> *Bodai nehan wa jōju shitamau*

All Buddhas and Bodhisattvas
  Achieve Buddhahood and Nirvana
As a result
  Of the Merciful Vow.

The Merciful Vow, as exemplified by Amida's Vow
to save all beings, renouncing Paradise until he has
done so, means the spirit of compassion and the desire
to rescue others from their sins. In other words, we
and the world are saved, in as far as we are loving In
what sense does Amida "renounce Paradise"? For us
it means giving up abstract truth for concrete error,
in giving up *satori* for attachment.

67.   仏性は不生不滅のものなれど
          まよへば生死流転とぞしれ

> *Busshō wa fushō fumetsu no mono naredo*
> *Mayoeba shōshi ruten tozo shire*

The Buddha-nature
  Means non-birth, non-extinction;
Then know that illusion
  Is birth, death, reincarnation.

All our life is a preparation for death,—not that
death is in itself so important, but because "the readiness is all," and this "readiness" is the Buddha-nature

68.   善修すれど悪事きたるとうらむなよ
          先世罪業卽為消滅

Zen shū suredo akuji kitaru to uramu na yo
Sense zaigō sokui shōmetsu

> Though you practise virtue,
> Do not grieve that misfortune arises;
> The guilty Karma
> Of the previous world
> Is vanishing away.

Grief and pain in this world is explained by the theory of reincarnation as the atonement for sins committed by us in previous lives. This explanation, which seems to stand or fall by an unacceptable doctrine of rebirth, has yet some independent validity in human experience, as we see when we compare it with the Christian doctrine of the vicarious suffering of Christ, and the members of the Church together with him. In other words the Christian idea is a mystical form of the Buddhist pseudoscientific notion.

69.　ふたつなきものとなりえて一もなし
　　　すみ絵の風のさてもすずしき

Futatsu naki mono to nari ete ichi mo nashi
Sumie no kaze no satemo suzushiki

> When they are not two things,
> They are not one thing,
> And the wind
> In the Indian-ink picture
> Is cool indeed.

When we think that the intellect is dichotomous and divides things into two, we suppose that the One is the reality. But this is not so. Things are empty in their self-nature, and therefore neither divisible into two nor reducible to a unity. When we "know" this, (and how seldom we do!) things are cool or warm, good or bad, according to the "picture" in our minds.

70.　死んでから仏といふもなにゆえぞ
　　　こゝともいはず邪魔にならねば

Shinde kara hotoke to iu mo nani yue zo
Kogoto mo iwazu jama ni naraneba

> Why are people called Buddhas
> After they die?
> Because they don't grumble any more,
> Because they don't make a nuisance
> Of themselves any more.

By this humorous verse Ikkyū seems to imply that if we merely live and let live even in this life we shall be Buddhas.

71.　月は家こゝろは主と見る時は
　　　なほかりの世のすまい也けり

Tsuki wa ie kokoro wa nushi to miru toki wa
　Nao kari no yo no sumai nari keri

> The moon is the house,
> The mind is the master in it:
> When we understand this,
> It is only a transitory world
> We live in here.

Our home is reality; he who dwells in it is God, is Buddha, is ourselves, our real self. Lawrence says in *Kangaroo*:

> Home again. But what was home? The fish has the vast ocean for home. And man has timelessness and nowhere. "I won't delude myself with the fallacy of home," he said to himself. "The four walls are a blanket I wrap around in, in timelessness and nowhere, to go to sleep."

The moon is "timelessness and nowhere"; the "fallacy of home" is the transitory world.

72.　おもひいれば人もわがみも他所ならず
　　　こゝろのほかに心なければ

Omoi ireba hito mo waga mi mo yoso narazu
　Kokoro no soto ni kokoro nakereba

> Deeply thinking of it,
> I and other people,—
> There is no difference,
> As there is no mind
> Beyond this Mind.

My mind is the Mind of All Things. Your mind is
the Mind of All Things. My mind and your mind is
the same mind, that is, your are I and I am you. In
the Christian vocabulary, it is the unqualified "rejoic-
ing with those that rejoice, and weeping with those
that weep."

73.　万法の行はよろづのことなれば
　　　こゝろこゝろに道をつとめよ

Bampō no gyō wa yorozu no koto nareba
Kokoro kokoro ni michi wo tsutome yo

> Since the activity of the Law
> 　Works manifoldly,
> Urge the following of the Way
> 　In various minds.

Our bodies grasp the variety of things; our minds
the unity. Only when the reverse *also* obtains, when
the body acts in the unity, and the mind is undismayed
at the cosmic confusion, do we get what Shelley found
in Wordsworth's poetry, "a sort of thought in sense."

74.　当来の三会の春の花もまた
　　　現世の慈悲ぞたねとならまし

Tōrai no san-e no haru no hana mo mata
Gense no jihi zo tane to naramashi

> The lovingkindness we feel,
> 　The merciful deeds we do in this life,
> Are the seeds of the spring flowers
> 　Of the future Third Meeting.

The "Third Meeting" means the appearance in the
infinitely distant future, of Miroku Bosatsu, Maitreya.
There seems here some implication that in our creation
of goodness we are the masters not of our own, but
of All Fate. Without us, the flower of eternity will
never bloom.

75.　身を入れて鳥けだものをすくひしは
　　　釈迦のいんちの修行なりけり

Mi wo irete tori kedamono wo sukuishi wa
Shaka no inchi no shugyō narikeri

    The salvation
Of birds and beasts, oneself included,—
    This is the object
Of Shakamuni's religious austerities
On the causal ground.

"On the causal ground" means the religious austerities performed by Shakamuni in former lives. For example, he was once a deer which stood in a river and enabled other animals to escape from a forest fire over his back. Lawrence says in *The Man Who Died*: "From what and to what could this infinite whirl be saved?" But, to answer him with his own words: "Life is what you want in your soul."

76. 春ごとに咲けるさくらを見るごとに
   なほはかなしと身こそつらけれ

Haru goto ni sakeru sakura wo miru goto ni
Nao hakanashi to mi koso tsurakere

    Every spring when you see
     The cherry blossoms bloom,
    Feel with pain
     The brevity of your life!

This verse has something morbid in it. The people who enjoy the cherry blossoms and the eating and drinking under them are perhaps wiser than the pseudo-poet who meditates on the ephemeral nature of things. "To catch the winged moment as it flies" is as important, to say the least of it, as to deplore its passing.

77. 元の身はもとのところへかへるべし
   いらぬ仏をたづねばしすな

Moto no mi wa moto no tokoro e kaeru beshi
Iranu hotoke wo tazune ba shisu na

    The original Man
     Must return to his original place;
    Why seek then
     The needless Buddha?

Death results from the persistent and increasing

desire to return to the state in which we were before
we were born. This state is the form of the Buddha
Nature. It is attained without any effort on our part.
Indeed our efforts only serve to hinder its attainment;
medicine, (the Buddha), cannot cure a healthy man,
rather it will do him harm.

78.　朝露はきえのこりてもありぬべし
　　　たれかこの世にのこりはつべき

Asatsuyu wa kie nokorite mo arinu beshi
Tareka kono yo ni nokori hatsu beki

> The morning dew
> Flees away,
> 　And is no more;
> Who may remain
> In this world of ours?

We feel in this verse the sadness of Buddhism which
brought out of the pleasure-loving Japanese the
melancholy that was latent in their hearts. And this
sadness is part of our inalienable heritage, the human
tragedy which makes *The Divine Comedy* look cheap.

79.　はかなくもあすの命をたのむかな
　　　きのふはすぎし心ならずや

Hakanaku mo asu no inochi wo tanomu kana
Kinō wa sugishi kokoro narazu ya

> We pray for our life of tomorrow,
> 　Ephemeral life though it be;
> This is the habit of our mind
> 　That passed away yesterday.

This waka expresses one of the oldest Buddhistic
ideas, that each person is a succession of fleeting selves,
with the illusion of continuance and permanence that
makes us "look before and after, and pine for what
is not." Where Buddhism makes its great mistake is
in asking for eternity without time. As Blake said:
"Eternity is in love with the productions of time."

80.　なげくなよまことの道はそのまゝに
　　　ふたつともなし三つともなし

Nageku nayo makoto no michi wa sono mama ni
Futatsu tomo nashi mittsu tomo nashi

Do not take it to heart;
    The real way
Is one, itself as it is;
    There are not two, or three.

Do not worry because you are a fool or a sinner.
Folly and wisdom, illusion and enlightenment, salvation and damnation are at bottom one thing. There
is in reality only one world, however we divide it
into scientific and poetic, finite and infinite, absolute
and relative.

HAKUIN'S COMMENTARY ON
THE *SHINGYŌ*

The usual name of this work is *Dokugo-chū Shingyō,*
literally "Poison word commentary pith sutra," that is
to say, a stinging, caustic explanation of the *Hannya
Haramita Shingyō,* in Sanskrit, *Prajnaparamita-Hridaya
Sutra.* When this latter was composed and by whom, is
not known. No doubt this was at more or less the same
time as the composition of the *Maka* (great) *Prajnaparamita Sutra,* which has 100,000 verses, the *Hridaya*
having only two hundred and sixty two characters in
the usual Chinese translation. Whether the one is a
condensation of the other, or vice versa an expansion,
is not easy to determine, and in any case "condensation" is not the right word, for *shin* means heart,
essence. The *Hridaya* was very popular in China, and
in Japan it is the most commonly chanted sutra in
the Zen Sect, together with the *Kannongyō* (*Samanta-
mukha-parivarta*) and the *Diamond Sutra* (*Kongō Kyō,
Vajracchedika*).

The translation generally used in China and Japan
is that by Hsuan-chuan (Genjō), the great Chinese
priest who started on his journey to India from the
capital Chang-an in 629 A.D. In about 632 he reached
Nalanda near Rajagriha, where Silabhadra, then a
hundred and six years old, was at the head of the
"university." Under him he studied the important
doctrines of Buddhism, especially those of Vasubandhu,
c. 420-500 A.D., and after seventeen years in India
returned to China in 645, and began his work as a
translator of the Buddhist canon. He was helped by
his disciple Kuei-chi (Kiki) 632-682, the actual
founder of the idealistic Fa-hsuang (Hossō) Sect. It
is noteworthy that the Japanese priest Dōshō, who
went to China in 653, studied under Hsuan-chuang,

living in the same room as Kuei-chi. He was the first
to convey the Hossō doctrines to Japan. The journey
to India of the translator of the *Hridaya* was made
the subject of the *Saiyūki,* a fabulous account of his
adventures together with a pig Hakkai, a water-spirit
Sagojō, and a monkey Songokū. Buddhist morals are
drawn from the incidents. This book was written by
an unknown author of the Ming Dynasty.

The *Hannya Shingyō* became and remained popular
because of its brevity, and because of its expression
of the essence of Buddhism. "Hannya" is wisdom, and
in these two hundred and sixty two Chinese characters
we are taught that all things are empty of self-nature,
and that when our mind has the same "emptiness" that
things have, we have then reached the "other shore,"
Nirvana, absolute and non-intellectual understanding,
wisdom. Having obeyed the command of the oracle,
we now "know ourselves." This realisation is the *shin,*
the "heart" of the "Great Wisdom."

The sutra has been translated into English by Suzuki
Daisetz in his *Manual of Zen Buddhism,* 1935, as follows:

> When the Bodhisattva Avalokitesvara was engaged
> in the practice of the deep Prajnaparamita, he per-
> ceived: there are the five Skandhas; and these he
> saw in their self-nature to be empty.
> "O Sariputra, form is here emptiness, emptiness is
> form; form is no other than emptiness, emptiness is
> no other than form; what is form that is emptiness,
> what is emptiness that is form. The same can be said
> of sensation, thought, confection, and consciousness.
> "O Sariputra, all things are here characterised with
> emptiness: they are not born, they are not an-
> nihilated; they are not stained, they are not im-
> maculate; they do not increase, they do not decrease.
> Therefore, O Sariputra, in emptiness there is no form,
> no sensation, no thought, no confection, no conscious-
> ness; no eye, ear, nose, tongue, body, mind; no form,
> sound, colour, taste, touch, objects; no Dhatu of vision,
> till we come to no Dhatu of consciousness; there is
> no knowledge, no ignorance, till we come to there is
> no old age and death; there is no suffering, accumula-

tion, annihilation, path; there is no knowledge, no attainment, (and) no realisation; because there is no attainment. In the mind of the Bodhisattva who dwells depending on the Prajnaparamita there are no obstacles; and, going beyond the perverted views, reaches final Nirvana, All the Buddhas of the past, present, and future, depending on the Prajnaparamita, attain to the highest perfect enlightenment.

"Therefore, one ought to know that the Prajnaparamita is the great Mantram, the Mantram of great wisdom, the highest Mantram, the peerless Mantram, which is capable of allaying all pain; it is truth because it is not falsehood: this is the Mantram proclaimed in the Prajnaparamita. It runs: 'Gate, gate, paragate, parasamgate, bodhi, bodhi, svaha!' (O Bodhi, gone, gone, gone to the other shore, landed at the other shore, Svaha)!'"

There are many commentaries on this sutra, by Dengyō-Daishi, Ikkyū Zenji, Kūkai, that is, Kōbō Daishi, and other monks great and small, but by far the best is that of Hakuin. Ikkyū's commentary is surprisingly feeble, conventional and indeed un-Zen-like. Hakuin's reminds us, in its trenchancy and vigour, of Rinzai's *Goroku*, Recorded Sayings.

In 1753 Hakuin had written his *jakugo* (notes) and *ju* (verses) on the *Shingyō*, and asked his disciple and successor Torei (Enji) to write a commentary on it. Somehow or other Hakuin's notes and verses and Torei's commentary seem to have been published separately, and this is a pity, because they complement each other. In 1863 Nantenbō, then a young monk, found a copy of Torei's commentary and later, in 1917, published these together with Hakuin's notes and poems. Hakuin's notes and verses are not so much an explanation of the sutra itself as an expression of Zen. They are Zen in words, just as silence must be Zen in silence, and our activity Zen in action. The sutra is an intellectual explanation of Zen; Hakuin is not explaining Zen, but speaking it, writing it. For the Anglo-Saxons, fighting was poetry (Zen) in action, and poetry (Zen) was fighting in words. So Hakuin's com-

ments and verses are not words about things, but words
which are things; they are not words with a separate
or separable meaning. They are to be swallowed, not
chewed. Thus any explanation we make of Hakuin's
comments and verses is turning them back again into
the original *Shingyō,* which is, except for the last few
lines, intellectual and unpoetical. As Dr. Suzuki points
out, it is only in these last lines, the mantra, that we
get the real McCoy, that pure, mindless, free, "poetic"
activity which is the soul of the sutra, as it is of
all true art, music, literature, and life. The following
is an account of the first few lines of the sutra, and
Hakuin's commentary. One sip of tea tells us the
taste of the whole cup.

Each phrase of the *Hannya Shingyō* is taken and
"praised" by abusing it. This abuse serves a double
purpose. It commends in reverse, and at the same time
prevents us from taking the Sutra too seriously, too
literally; we are reminded at every step that truth
exists only in so far as we do not keep it fixed in
words or principles or habits or creeds. At the beginning there is a short passage of introduction followed
by a verse, which serves to give the tone of Hakuin's
(Buddhistically) blasphemous justification of the way
of no God to non-existent men.

Introductory Commentary and Verse:

A blind old chap, full of mental entanglements and
in the darkness of emotional confusion, sits in the
grasses, not a stitch of clothing on him.[1] Poor old
Priest Fu ![2] He has lost all his grand palaces. But
do not say that this sutra is thin and tasteless ! One
mouthful of reality relieves an eternal hunger.

---

1. This blindness, irrationality, and nakedness is our natural
and proper condition, if only we knew it. The "old chap" is
Kannon (and also Hakuin himself).

2. A priest of the same period as Daruma, 6th century, supposed to be an incarnation of Miroku Bosatsu, the Buddha of the
future. Hakuin says ironically, that Kannon has put Miroku
Bosatsu's nose out of joint, making him unnecessary.

Throw this luxuriant entangling growth[3] that fills
   all the sky
Over all the great monks of the Four Seas and
   Five Lakes,[4] and tie them up.[5]
I beg you, find the way to free movement,
So that you may hawk at your pleasure in the inter-
   stices of a lotus root.[6]

The *Hannya Shingyo,* and Hakuin's commentary on
it, are equally words, not real life. But you must find
your freedom in these very restrictions, in the *trivia*
of life. You must be bound by Hakuin's commentary,
and yet free of it. In the willing, not doing, of the
impossible, the impossible is achieved. Everything is
will, everything is subjective. Stop thinking about the
why and wherefore of life. Cease wanting this, and
not wanting that. It is foolish to fear death all your
life, and die anyway at the end of it. Don't read the
philosophers and the sages and saints, or try to solve
all the Zen problems, the meaning of *Mu* and of the
sound of the clapping of one hand, and all that nonsense. Be free of them and of all things, so that you
can play the piano nonchalantly and incompetently
before an audience of ten thousand, and be buried alive
with equanimity and boredom.

MAKA

Comment

   This is translated "great" in Chinese, but what
does it really mean? It is impossible to compare this
"great" to the four corners of the universe, or the
whole height and depth of the cosmos. Many people

---

   3. This commentary of Hakuin's.

   4. Of the world.

   5. Hakuin is boasting that he can do this, but also warning
readers against himself.

   6. The root of the lotus has small holes running through it.
Inside these small dark sticky holes you must be able to go hawk-
ing, and enjoy it. There is an interesting use of a similar metaphor
in *Macbeth.* Donalbain says to Malcolm, when they fear what may
happen to them after the murder of their father:

   What should be spoken here, where our fate
   Hid in a auger-hole, may rush, and seize us?

have misunderstood this "great" as vastness, mere
size. Even a sage needs the necessities of life, but
he knows the right way to get them [so I will tell
you how to get this "great" Wisdom]. But just try
and bring me a "small" Wisdom !

Hakuin says that this term "great" is easily taken
in its material sense. Actually, real wisdom cannot
be called great or small; it is transcendental and incapable of comparison; indeed, no epithets can or
should be applied to it. Just as the Godhead is nameless and nounless, so It is adjectiveless (and capital-
or-small-letter-less).

Verse

A million Mount Sumerus[7] are but a drop of dew
    on the end of a single hair;
Three thousand worlds are only a sea-gull floating
    on the ocean waves.
The two children of the tiny creatures in the eye-
    brows of a mosquito
Never stop quarrelling between themselves as to
    whose this earth is.[8]

In this verse Hakuin Zenji is trying to show us once
more that "great" has no spacial or temporal or indeed
any spiritual meaning. All is relative, that is to say,
of no absolute size, length of time, or value. We must
especially beware of such simple words as "in." "To
see a world *in* a grain of sand," is to see the world
and the grain of sand as one thing, the whole being
just as much *in* the part as the part is *in* the whole.

All through the *Dokugo-chū Shingyō*. Hakuin keeps
up this bantering tone. It is odd that the truth can
be expressed only in this way. "Lightness is all."
"Levity is the soul of wit." All the revues and cabarets
and masquerades in the world are an adumbration of
this truth.

---

7. Mount Sumeru, a kind of Buddhist Olympus, is the highest
mountain of every world. At the top is Indra's heaven and around
it are the four devalokas, realms of the gods; surrounding these
are eight circles of mountains, and the eight seas.

8. They both claim it as their own.

THE SAYINGS OF RENNYO SHŌNIN

That the Nembutsu, the repetition of the name of Buddha is in some way the same, fundamentally, as zazen, was realised quite early in the history of (Chinese) Buddhism. "Namuamidabutsu" is a sort of zazen of the mouth; zazen is a kind of Namuamidabutsu with the legs. Modesty and power; these two contradictory essentials were respectively stressed by the "other-power" and "self-power" temperaments of human nature, and formed themselves into groups "at the ringing of a bell." Modesty is pure modesty. Comparisons are odious, but you are something, I am nothing. I am only the powerless eye which sees your modesty, your power. Power is pure power, not power over others. It is the power to see your modesty and power, your power to see my powerlessness. In this confusion of words, power and modesty approach each other, and for a moment are seen as two names of one nameless thing. So *jiriki* and *tariki*, self-power and other-power, might be re-named other-modesty and self-modesty. It is the region of the Upanishads, "You are It, It is you." Elation and depression, centrifugal and centripetal, everything is made of these two forces.

In Japan even Zen has been modest, except to some extent in its Bushidō aspect. Jōdoshū and Shinshū appealed to the under-dog, the outcast, the slave in all but name, as did early Christianity. But after all, is the super-man really so fine? Even Abraham Lincoln owes his (false) prestige to the tears and groans of the Civil War. Is it so laudable to torture and kill a large number of human beings for the sake of some abstractions and ideals that will be realised, if ever, in the remote future? As Sidney Smith said,

199

The world is bursting with sin and sorrow. Am I to be a champion of the Decalogue, and to be everlastingly raising fleets and armies to make all men good and happy?

There was enough humour and poetry and humanity in the Japanese character to make Shinshū as satisfying to those who were modest and wanted to be more modest, as Zen was to those who had some (real) power, and wanted still more. From the time of Hōnen and Shinran, men with a genius for humility appeared one after another, though history takes but little notice of them. They were often compromising, narrow-minded, patriotic, superstitious, even fanatical, but the underlying thought of no ambition, no wealth, no fame, no glory, saved them from all but the smaller faults. Pride is sin; sin is pride.

The *Ichidaiki Kikigaki*, literally, "The Writing of Things Heard about a Life," is 316* short anecdotes and pithy sayings of Rennyo, the 8th Patriarch of Shinshu, and of people of his circle, as recorded by Jitsugo, one of his sons. Jitsugo is said to have been Rennyo's twelfth son (though my calculations make him the eleventh) born when his father was seventy seven, eight years old at his father's death. Rennyo was married five times and had twenty seven children in all, thirteen daughters and fourteen sons.

Before we speak of Rennyo himself it will be better to consider the times in which he lived and the religious stream to which he was tributary. At the end of the 8th century and the beginning of the ninth, two great Japanese priests, Kōbō Daishi, 774-835, and Dengyō Daishi, 767-822, were trying to bring happiness and prosperity to Japan through Buddhism. This aim appeared 400 years later in the super-patriotism of Nichiren, 1222-1282, but there were two other elements latent in the Buddhism of Kōbō and Dengyō, the

---

* In *Kōsō Meicho Senshū, vol. 13, Rennyo Shōnin*, there are 313 anecdotes.

practical transcendentalism of Zen and the other-worldliness of Jōdo and Shin. The first of these became distinct in Eisai, 1141-1215, and Dōgen, 1200-1225; and the second in Hōnen, 1133-1212, and Shinran, 1173-1262. We may add in passing that it was perhaps Zen which won the battle between three main divisions of Japanese Buddhism, especially during the Sengoku period, 1467-1600, which ended with the consolidation of political power by Ieyasu and the proscription of Christianity. Rennyo was born in 1415, and lived until 1498, in a period of that internecine warfare which seems productive of both types of religious activity, monastic and militant.

Hōnen had taught, basing himself on Zendō, 613-681, the great Chinese teacher of the Pure Land doctrine, that Amida's one way of salvation was the whole-hearted and ceaseless repetition of the Buddha's name. According to Shinran, the repetition is not so much a means of salvation as an expression of gratitude on the part of the believer. With Ippen, 1239-1289, the founder of the Ji sect, faith in Amida is not what saves us. We are simply saved by Amida, that is all. The idea of this act-state of being nothing, in which "there is neither myself nor the Buddha," shows the effect of Zen, which appears more strongly in Ryōyo Shōgei, 1341-1420, the seventh patriarch of the Jōdo sect, who taught that Paradise is right here and now. Rennyo's additions to and developments of the Pure Land doctrine were his insistence upon obedience to the laws of morality, and rendering unto Caesar the things which are Caesar's; and his teaching that all the Shintō deities were appearances of the Buddha, and that when we call on the name of the Buddha all the Shintō gods are included therein, it being thus unnecessary to worship these latter in their Shintō forms.

Many of the sayings of Rennyo are a strange mixture of the sharpness of Zen and the softness of Shinshū.

This sharpness or tartness may be seen in No. 5, which says:

> Rennyo Shōnin quoted to someone the paradox: "Break in pieces the image of Buddha; tear up the Scriptures !"

Another example is No. 50:

> Once he said to a large and earnest audience: "I wonder how many of you are going to receive the gift of faith; one or two at most, I suppose." They were all dumbfounded by this.

Besides these touches of Zen there is something Christian and something modern about Rennyo. Like Christ, he says that we don't go to hell because we are sinners, but because we think we are not (No. 58). There is here also some connection with Greek philosophers: wisdom is knowledge of our ignorance; religion is a knowledge of our wickedness. Again, Rennyo admired what might be called fanaticism in the same way that Cardinal Newman did. The English priest says: "I will not shrink from uttering my firm conviction, that it would be a gain to this country were it vastly more superstitious, more bigoted, more gloomy, more fierce in its religion, than at present it shows itself to be." What the Japanese priest says is not so hard, not so dark, more humorous, but just as earnest, in No. 62:

> There was a man of the province of Settsu called Gunke no Kazue. Incessantly repeating the Nembutsu, he always cut himself while shaving; he forgot everything but the Nembutsu.

There is a deeper meaning in the following, No. 73:

> Hōshō of Kyuhōji asked Rennyo: "Is it a fact that we are saved by once asking Amida for salvation? Is it really so?" Someone present there said," That's such a hackneyed question; ask something else." Rennyo said, "No, no. It is wrong to ask about some recondite matter. We should ask again and again,

as Hōshō did, revealing the desire of our heart concerning matters of faith."

Milton divorced his wife for being silent, and Rennyo
would have sympathised with him. In No. 86 is says:

> Rennyo was always telling people to express them-
> selves. "A man who is silent is to be feared. Whether
> you are a believer or not, just speak your mind. If
> you do that you will be known, and your errors
> corrected. Just talk!"

Again in No. 74 we have:

> It's quite all right for a man to say he is an un-
> believer, but to pretend to religion in words and
> appearance, and be hypocritical and empty, this is
> a sorry state indeed.

In *The Age of Reason,* Tom Paine expresses this more
precisely:

> Infidelity does not consist in believing or disbeliev-
> ing; it consists in professing to believe what one does
> not believe.

This being so, our teacher must be, as Rennyo says
in Nos. 16 and 168, anyone who really believes, not
the "professional good men" as Sinclair Lewis calls
priests and parsons in *Elmer Gantry.* To know means
to be grateful, Rennyo thinks. Gratitude is the first
(and last) step to truth, No. 213; and in No. 211 Rennyo
tells us he found it hard to die, from his fervent desire
to arouse faith in those many who did not have it.

Rennyo wrote a hundred and sixty odd waka, or
dōka, not very interesting on the whole,—but let us
take leave of this most interesting fifteenth century
character by quoting what is perhaps the best of them.
His love of Amida, the worshipped, almost overflows
onto himself, the worshipper, reminding us of the
Sponsa Dei of Coventry Patmore.

彌陀たのむ我が身の心の尊とさに
　　いつも涙に濡るる袖かな

Mida tanomu waga mi no kokoro no tōtosa ni
Itsu mo namida ni nururu sode kana

How grateful I am
For this heart of mine that trusts
In Amida for salvation !
My sleeves are wet always
At the mere thought of it.

ZEN AND THE OBJECT OF LIFE

To attain a state of Zen, to live by Zen may well seem to be the object of life, "life" in this case meaning mere existence. Strictly speaking, however, mere existence could have no object; we must move from meaning to meaning, not from meaningless to meaningful. Thus we ask the question, what is the object of Zen, not of Zen training, but Zen itself? It is our human nature to ask questions which apparently should not be asked. Why is a blackboard black? Why is a soft thing softer than a thing less soft? Why can't we have a cause without an effect?

It is an odd trait of human nature also, and not so commendable, to put the cart before the horse, to put the Sabbath before man, the State before the citizen, Zen before (sexual) love and affection. In the history of the world men have used women, and women have used men, for their own purposes, so they supposed, but what really happened? It is possible to go from unrequited affection to Zen. Thoreau says, "All nature is my bride," and this means loving and being loved by Nature, which is a definition of Zen, but Thoreau also says something which sounds truer and deeper, "The only remedy for love is to love more," and "more" is qualitative, not quantitative. What I want to suggest now is the heterodox, not to say heretical idea, that the aim of Zen is to bring two people, preferably of the opposite sex, together, in other words, that the function of Zen is to remove the impediments to the marriage of true minds.

The theory of the matter is this. Two persons, heterosexual by (Nature's) preference, must have, or better, must be going to have the same feelings and thoughts about everything in the world, including themselves

and one another. It should be noted that the feelings
must be proper, and the thoughts right. It's no good
having the same cruelty or the same stupidity. (What
"proper" and "right" means is easy to explain. It is
what I myself think is right and proper, today; tomorrow of course I shall think differently.) To be more
specific, these two imaginary people must love Bach
and Bashō and Po Chüi and Eckhart and Cervantes
and El Greco and animals and plants and the round
ocean and the living air,—in the same way; this is the
catch. Further, and equally important, they must hate
the same things and the same persons, for the same
reasons. I forgot to mention the most important part,
the sexual parts. The two people must be in love with
each other's bodies, the appetite growing with what it
feeds on. All this is the ideal, and in the case of the
real, each incongruity of attitude, every nuance of dis-
similar feeling, all differences of judgement are to be
felt as iron entering into the soul. A never-resting
eagerness to enter into the other person's hopes and
fears, a constant determination never to deceive oneself
into seeing non-existent identities, and never to close
the eyes to patent dissimilarities,—this is the essence
of such a pair.

The objection to this 50 year plan are three: that
it is impossible; it would be monotonous; and it is
exhaustingly over-intense. As for its impossibility, this
may be admitted; like peace on earth, and going to
heaven, and the understanding of Zen, they are the
heart's desire, and very easy not to achieve. But an
ideal is something that however little we approach
it, that little is what makes life worth living. The
novels of the world are the accounts of the non-
attainment of this union of souls.

The second objection, the monotonousness of such a
condition, is also a valid one, but Nature kindly
prevents all possibility of such ennui by making our
span of life far too short to attain it. In addition, the
differences of sex, nationality, environment, education

and so on make the whole business so fantastic that monotony is the last objection to be made against it.

The third objection also, that it requires an enormous amount of nervous energy, that it is too conscious, too unnatural, involves us in ceaseless self-analysis and comparison,—this is only too true. Byron says that even love must have rest, and Thoreau that our best relations are buried under a positive depth of silence. But what is the alternative? Laziness, indifference, unloved, unloving loneliness, unknown, unknowing insensitiveness, infinity, eternity, happiness,—I had almost written Zen. What is the alternative to the alternative? Hours of anguish, moments of blessedness; mutual suspicion, mutual trust; withdrawal from the world; for all married and unmarried people, looking at anything and everything as Wordsworth and Dorothy did the glow-worm:

> Oh! joy it was for her, and joy for me!

And when Romeo dies, Juliet cannot live; when Juliet dies Romeo must die too.

What is Zen? Zen is looking at things with the eye of God, that is, becoming the thing's eyes so that it looks at itself with our eyes. But this is not enough. Impression must always be accompanied by expression. Impression without expression is not yet impression. Expression without impression is impossible. Impression and expression are both parts of "pression." But impression and expression are not enough. Expression without reception is meaningless. It is not expression if it is to nobody. This is why all art, all music, all poetry requires two persons. Why only two? How can you ask for a crowd, when even two minds with the same thought is almost unheard-of? At best, life is a triangle albeit an imperfect one, Wordsworth, Dorothy, Nature. Wordsworth and the glow-worm is not enough. Dorothy and the glow-worm is even less satisfactory. "Nothing is fair or good alone." The three are necessary.

I wish to take *The Glow-worm* as a test case to decide

whether Zen is an end or a means, that is, whether the object of life is union with Nature, or whether it is union with another person. Here is *The Glow-worm*:

> Among all lovely things my Love had been;
> Had noted well the stars, all flowers that grew
> About her home; but she had never seen
> A Glow-worm, never one, and this I knew.

> While riding near her home one stormy night
> A single Glow-worm did I chance to espy;
> I gave a fervent welcome to the sight,
> And from my Horse I leapt; great joy had I.

> Upon a leaf the Glow-worm did I lay,
> To bear it with me through the stormy night:
> And, as before, it shone without dismay;
> Albeit putting forth a fainter light.

> When to the Dwelling of my Love I came,
> I went into the Orchard quietly;
> And left the Glow-worm, blessing it by name,
> Laid safely by itself, beneath a Tree.

> The whole next day, I hoped, and hoped with fear;
> At night the Glow-worm shone beneath the Tree:
> I led my Lucy to the spot, "Look here."
> Oh ! joy it was for her, and joy for me !

The question is: did Wordsworth want his sister to be with him so that he could see the glow-worm poetically, or did he want to look at the glow-worm together with her so as to be at one with her? (It may be called a case of the hen and the egg, but the problem is not which came first in time, but which comes first in value.) The glow-worm is the universe, the wonderful world we live in. Zen is the life of wonder. Really to look at the glow-worm is Zen. But without Dorothy the glow-worm is nothing, that is, nothing in itself. Dorothy is something in herself, but without the glow-worm love is only potential. Love means looking at the same thing with the same eye, not looking at each other with different eyes. The glow-worm is nothing, the universe is nothing, Zen is nothing. The only important thing for you is me,

the only important thing for me is you. How do we
know this? We know it by intuition, but we may also
remember Oscar Wilde's words, "I like persons better
than principles, and I like persons with no principles
better than anything else the world."

To make the matter clearer, let us compare *The
Glow-worm* with Bashō's *Furu ike ya*:

> The old pond;
> A frog jumps in,
> The sound of the water.

Here we have no triangle of man, woman, and nature.
Even man himself is present, if at all, in the sound
of the water. Bashō is not seen, even in imagination,
looking down at the pond, or with ear attentive. Man
is swallowed up in nature, woman is not worthy even
of being forgotten, or absent; she has no existence.
The aim of Bashō is achieved when he becomes the
ear by which the water hears itself. Or is Bashō
perhaps a kind of woman, who does not need another
one; or is he a hermaphrodite? But the law still holds,
impression, expression, reception. Who receives? In
the case of Wordsworth and Dorothy the reception is
mutual. With Bashō it must be himself, or humanity
imagined, that is, involved in the Zen experience.

The question is, which is better, ("better" means
deeper) the a-sexual, Japanese Zen experience, or the
sexual, English Zen experience? Actually, the frog
jumping into the water and making a sound is as
Freudian a symbol as one could hope to find, even more
so than the contractile, soft glow-worm with its green
fire of love. Gutei's finger held up (and significantly
cut off) in *Mumonkan* III, the monk raising his fist,
XI, Nansen killing the cat, XIV; Unmon's shit-stick,
XXI; Ryutan's blowing out the candle, XXVIII; Jōshu's
oak tree, XXXVII; the tail that remains behind,
XXXVIII; Isan's tipping over the water-pot, XXXX;

---

1. The pond is old because a prostitute of 30 is far more exciting than a virgin of 20.

Shuzan's short staff, XXXXIII; Bashō's staff, XXXXIV; Sekiso's jumping from the top of a pole, XXXXVI; all these are obviously sexually symbolic. Zen cannot escape from sex, except by ignoring it, that is, by transcending it. But we cannot annihilate a thing by transcending it. Religion has always omitted women, as it has omitted nature, and human nature, but the result has been that religion has omitted itself.

If the matter is to be decided according to its scale, Bashō's sound of the water, which is the word of God, is vast and all-including. Wordsworth and Dorothy's rather suspiciously passionate love of each other seems insignificant by comparison. But "Eternity is in love with the productions of time." Gempō Rōshi said that the murder of time is the greatest sin. Alice was told by the Hatter that she must not beat time. Take care of the pence of time, and the pounds of eternity will take care of themselves. The universe is a thought by which I think of you, and you think of me. If we think different thoughts, if our universes are different, if we are all Robinson Crusoes, each on his own desert island....

ZEN AND REALITY

What is the relation between Zen and reality? But what is reality? How can we know it? Even if, as the Greeks supposed, man is a microcosmos corresponding more or less exactly to the macrocosmos, or as the ancient Indians put it, "You are It," we still have to know ourselves, and when we have done this, we have to know the knower of ourselves, which by definition is impossible. How can we know God before He knew any thing, before there was anything to know, before the creation of the universe, before the creation of all the other universes, if any?

To put the question in quite a different way,—is there something besides Zen? Is there something "real" which is not covered by the word Zen, if we use it in the sense of *meaning*? Zen is the resolution of two intellectually incompatible facts. The table is a table, and Zen will not deny it. But it will assert also that the table is not a table, and go further, linking the two contradictory facts by, "The table is a table because it is not a table." The question we are asking here does not go so far as this. It asks whether the "fact" that the moon is a lifeless clod of stone, and the "fact" that it "doth with delight look round it when the heavens are bare," are equal or not. "Equal" means equal in power, in validity, in inevitability, equally capable of being controlled by us. Macbeth asks, "Will all great Neptune's ocean wash this blood clean from my hand?" and answers rightly that it will not. The sea is not merely H_2O+sodium chloride. But can the poetic imagination, that is Zen, imagine the H_2O+salt away? It can add (tragic) meaning to it, can see it different in colour (green or red), touch it differently, be drowned in it differently, but it is always there, not potentially, but actually, whereas what the hand of Macbeth in-carnadines is there potentially, not actually.

According to Buddhism and Berkeley, all is in the mind, but this begs the question. You cannot kick a stone out of existence, as Dr. Johnson unwittingly demonstrated, but neither can you think it out of existence. "Nothing is good or bad, but thinking makes it so." This is true, but we cannot say, "A stone does not exist, or not-exist, but thinking makes it so," as far as our own thinking is concerned. If it is said that the stone exists in the mind of God, in the Dharmakaya, it is only saying that there are thoughts in the mind of God that nobody can unthink.

Zen is the resolution of absolute freedom and in-vincible law. But obedience is unlimited; liberty is not. Zen asserts that when a horse in one country eats grass, the stomach of a cow in another country is filled. This is true, because I am both the horse and the cow, and the grass too, and the batsman and the bat, but there is some swindling here, because the fact that I am I is a different, a stronger kind of fact than the fact that I am a cow or coconut. If I assert that there is a wall before me, that is all right, but if I say there is no wall and keep on trying to walk through it I shall find myself given three more, all padded.

We must say then that there is, besides Zen, a sub-stratum of fact, brute fact, and not pretend that by levitation, or will-power, or thought-transference, or poetic insight, or mystic ecstasy, it can be un-facted. Zen can make us lose the fear of death (though whether it should, is another question) but "the inevitable hour" is unavoidable. We live in time; we live timelessly, and these two are the same, but they are also different. Time is our only chance to live in eternity. "A night cometh, in which no man can work."

The mistake which Zen has made is in wishfully be-lieving that minds can be one though bodies are not. Body and mind are indissolubly united. They are identical. "That called body is a portion of soul dis-

cerned by the five senses"; Blake should rather have
written, "Body is soul seen by the senses." If two bodies
are two, the minds are two. Sexual intercourse is the
vain attempt to break this law and unite what God
hath put asunder.

The microcosmos cannot become the macrocosmos
physically; this body of mine is not that of the insect
that crosses the page, or of the sun that shines upon
it. My spirit and the universal spirit can have only
an illusion of oneness. This illusion is of course better
than nothing, better than the intolerable loneliness of
each microcosmos in its physico-spiritual isolation from
all the other physico-spiritual entities. It is what makes
life bearable. God made the mistake of thinking, thinking something different from himself. These thoughts
of His started business on their own account, thinking
their own thoughts, and the aim of Zen was to rectify
the original error, turn back the wheels of time, and
return us to the state of innocence from which we fell
into experience. But we have learned the painful sweetness of our *mayoi*. We know the pleasures of masochism
and sadism. Zen, it is true, promises us, saying that
satori is *mayoi*, that "all these things shall be added
unto you," the power and the glory, the misery and
despair, but "Only what everyone believes is so," and
the common sense of humanity doubts its ability to
become God.

> If the Sun and Moon should doubt,
> They'd immediately go Out.

This is true, but the moon was extinguished long, long
ago, the Sun is going out, and we must all follow suit.
What Zen lacks is "the modesty of Nature." By that
sin fell the angels. It may be difficult for God to be
modest, for Zen to admit its limitations, but our faith
is in what St. Paul calls "the foolishness of God," a
Zen that will confess its sins.

Zen makes the mistake of speaking two languages,
and does not distinguish between them; only occasional-

ly does it speak a third, which it should speak always
The first is the language of science, of (un)common
sense. "When tired, we rest; when hungry, we eat."
"A dog has the Buddha nature." It is the language of
the relative world. The second is that of paradox,
nonsense, mysticism. "When a horse in Essex eats, the
stomach of a cow in Devonshire is filled." "A dog has
not the Buddha nature." This is the language of the
absolute world.

The third language is the real language of Zen, of
poetry; it is the relative and absolute in one. It is the
language of art and music and great deeds, Gutei cutting off the finger of his disciple, the man at the top
of a pole who must go higher.

We say, "I have a pebble in my right hand"; Zen
may add, "You have (also) a no-pebble in your right
hand," or, "You have also a pebble in your (empty)
left hand," but this is not, strictly speaking, the language
of Zen, for it is not poetry. "The essence of Zen is
enlightenment." This is commonsense and scientific.
But if we say (remembering that enlightenment is
illusion), "The essence of Zen is illusion," this is still
only half the truth, the paradoxical half. That is to
say, Zen should assert, "The essence of Zen is enlightenment," only if the listener or reader is forewarned that
this means "Zen is (also) illusion," or, "Zen is
enlightenment and illusion when they are one," or,
"Zen is enlightenment and illusion when they are both
two and one." "Zen has no God-concept" must mean,
"Zen has (also) a God-concept." Further, an ordinary
statement may be, by the speaker or to the hearer,
poetry, and conversely, poetry, if read badly becomes
an ordinary statement or worse. Paradoxes, when
uttered in cold blood, are repulsively insincere, but
paradoxes may also be poetry:

> And 'tis my faith that every flower
> Enjoys the air it breathes.

Zen should speak the language of paradox only when it is poetical.

Going back to the original subject, Zen and Reality, when Zen opens its mouth in the ordinary way, it must warn the hearer that it is going to put its foot into it. Zen cannot explain itself rationally, that is, dichotomously without being false to itself. But it may go so far as to distinguish the spiritual freedom of our *attitude* to things, and the unresolvably determined nature of the *thing itself*. It must point out that we are the masters of our fate, but in two distinct ways. First, we can think and feel what we please about things. Second, we can be willingly obedient to the unchangeable will of nature. "Love's not time's fool." This is true, but neither is time the fool of love.

I once asked Dr. Suzuki Daisetz the question proposed before, "What will happen to you when you die?" He answered, "I shall go out of existence, I think,— but the desire for a future life is also a fact!" Reality is thus of two kinds, and Zen deals with the second, the second only. It can cure a broken heart, but not a broken neck. Zen is the greatest thing in the world, —after reality. We pray for our daily bread; bread gives us the strength to do so.

NO JAPANESE ZEN, THANK YOU!

The other day I asked a rōshi what he would do for the rest of the day (it was about three in the afternoon) if he knew he was going to die that night. Before he had time to answer I suggested he might listen to Bach's music; or look at a collection of masterpieces of Occidental and Oriental paintings; or go next door and hold the baby while the mother went to the cinema. He answered that he would do zazen. On my suggesting that he might do something for humanity before he left it behind in all its confusion and misery, he said that his doing zazen would be of inestimable value to the whole world, far more than any acts of virtue could be. In support of this idea he gabbled off something from Dōgen which I could not understand, but which I felt to be an argumentum ad baculum. This notion I had not heard before in Zen, though the Juzunembutsu, and the Protestant idea of the efficacy of prayer, and Roman Catholic prayers for the dead were of course familiar to me.

One other example, before I come to my thesis. I asked the rōshi, as I have asked several others, what was going to happen to him when he died. To make the answer easy for him, I told him how I had put the same question to a woman rōshi in Kyōto. She answered that she wasn't going anywhere, and when I said I would go with her, she was very pleased, partly perhaps because she was a spinster of eighty who had obviously never yet been anywhere with a man. The rōshi, the man, I mean, agreed with this, and I supposed that he meant what I did, that death is the end of all existence of a personal kind, in other words, "There is no knowledge nor wisdom in the grave, whither thou goest," but he then began to talk about transmigration, and how he would come back and go on doing zazen as before. Also, that Dōgen and so on still existed in some way or other, so we make offerings to their spirits and ask for their assistance when in any kind of difficulty, spiritual or physical.

There are two points I want to make: first, that Zen must have nothing oriental or occidental, Buddhist or Christian, masculine or feminine about it; second, that only satori, that is, deep experience, is true.

To begin with the second point, the mistake we all make is to confuse what we know with what we don't know. We know, for example, that the sun rose today, but we don't know it will rise tomorrow. In England thirty years ago, famous cricketers used to be asked their opinion about the existence of the Deity, the idea being that a man who could hit eight fours and three sixes in one innings must also have theological, not to say mystical intuitions. This kind of mistake, which everyone makes, is also made by Zen-enlightened people. They do not distinguish what they know by enlightenment, and what they (think they) know by education, custom, personal prejudice and so on. Enlightenment does not reveal to us anything which happened in the past or which will happen in the future. Enlightenment is being caught up in this moment which is both in time and beyond time. In being beyond time it partakes of the past and the future, and with regard to events of the past and future we can, or should be able to, make better guesses, think more clearly about them, but that is all. Zen speaks only of this moment. Indeed, Zen is this moment speaking. Thus, if we are asked what will happen to us after death, Zen does not answer,—let us be more courageous, and say that Zen *cannot* answer, just as God cannot tell a lie.

Zen theory distinguishes between *dai-ichi-gi,* and *dai-ni-gi,* between the absolute and relative, and we may speak from either. For example, absolutely speaking, men and women are the same, and their enlighten-

ment is the same; but relatively speaking, they are
different, and their enlightenment is different. But Zen
means speaking from both at the same time, and we
must speak from both at same time all the time. Thus
Zen cannot assert either the mortality or the immortality, the existence or the non-existence of the
soul. Buddhism may do so, for it is a religion; Christianity may do so, it is a religion; Zen cannot so do,
because it is religion itself, which deals with the infinite
in this finite place, eternity at this moment of time, and
cannot make general or abstract statements about any
world to come or not to come. What answer shall we
give then to the question, "Is there an after-life?"
Thoreau's is the most concise: "One world at a time !"

To come to the second point, there is nothing
American (Christian) about this answer, and when a
Japanese rōshi replies, he should reply in the same
unjapanese way. Above all, we do not want the
casuistry and sophistry of the double answer, that from
the absolute point of view we are unborn and undying,
as far as our real self is concerned; and from the relative
viewpoint we are blessed or cursed with a succession
of rebirths and redeaths. If I am asked the question
(and I never am), I will say that, upon dispassionate
inspection, the life of man looks like that of the plants,
that grow, reach maturity, decay, and disintegrate into
their various elements. This is doubtless the law for
the so-called spiritual world, which actually is not
separate from or even correlated with the material
world, but is a mere aspect of it, just as the material
world is a mere aspect of the spiritual. This answer,
however, is not the kind of answer I give when asked
about Bach's *Art of Fugue,* or Bashō's *Furu ike ya,*
or Shakespeare's "Never, never, never, never, never."
It is only an opinion, and per se no better than anybody
else's.

Japanese people must read *King Lear* with all the
depth and tragic integrity and poetry they can summon
up. English people are to read *Oku no Hosomichi* with

all the sublime simplicity and purity and religiousness
they can muster. In the same way, Japanese Zen is
to be the experience of Japanese people of their
humanity, that is, the sound of water, the taste of tea,
the bending of branches, the look of food on a plate,
the realisation that all's right with this terrible world.
There is no superstition or dogma or provincialism, no
wishful thinking, nothing that stinks of India or China
or Japan here. The Zen which is the essence of
Christianity must in the same way leave behind the
Virgin Birth, the divinity of Christ, the existence or
non-existence of God. These things may and should
all be kept as symbols, not of ineffable mysteries, but
of our own virginity, our own divinity, our own existence, and our own non-existence.

   Zen is the poetry of life, and all poetry is the same,
all poetry is different. The joy at the sameness, the
joy at the difference, this is ZEN. And beyond this
there is doubtless another Zen, but the printer can't
print it, yet.

POSTSCRIPT

It will have been painfully and indignantly obvious to the reader that the word Zen has been used in this book in a variety of ways, sometimes as employed by the Zen sect with a mystical meaning; sometimes as a sort of religious humbug; at times as universal culture, at times as the particular enlightenment of an individual; at others with a prophetic meaning, a Zen which may be attained by poetical persons who see things with an Eastern and a Western eye, who can be both non-sexual and sexual, atheists who can be God. In any case, Zen is not something that changes and grows; it is the changing and growing itself, and if anybody (or any thousand million bodies) thinks that Zen is something to be gained by doing zazen and receiving Zen diplomas, he is mistaken. If anybody supposes that Buddha or Daruma or Rinzai attained to Zen, he is mistaken. If anybody imagines that Christ or any other man born after him was a Christian, he is mistaken. Look at Jesus. He was perhaps homosexual. Well, I don't care for it, but to love a louse or the leg of a chair and have sexual intercourse with it is all right with me. For goodness sake be fond of somebody or something! Jesus loved one of his disciples especially. That is why he cried from the cross, "Oh, John; oh, John, why have you forsaken me?" (I suppose John was boozing in a bar.) Jesus also drank, drank the cup which his Father gave him to drink. This was Jōshu's cup: "Have a cup of Zen tea!" It was the cup which nobody drank in the Black Hole of Calcutta, twenty two feet square, in which 146 prisoners were confined; only twenty three were alive in the morning.

What is the Zen I am now talking about? Zen is our feeling of "grief," something which is not an emotion, but which even the so-called enlightened man may experience at the serenity of Bach, the humour of Dickens, the joy of Wordsworth, the no-regret of Thoreau, the *Paradiso* of Dante. Man wishes to be immortal, but he is not. He consoles himself with eternity, but timelessness itself needs time, and time is limited. "The moon is setting with me, O!" To escaped from his finiteness he identifies himself with the rest of the universe, but this involves his finiteness in an infinity of suffering, for even apparently inanimate things all suffer, in being what they are, and in not being what they are not. "The whole creation groaneth and travaileth in pain...waiting...." Thus the life of the "sons of God" is a tragic, an hourly tragedy, only deeper than that of all other creatures. But this "grief" at a willow-tree swaying in the breeze, at a national anthem, at a mountain cuckoo, at the redemption of man, is not an end in itself. It is something for you and me to experience alone, and to experience together. As Hamlet did not say, though it might be another name for the play, "Togetherness is all."

One last thing remains to say about Zen, the most difficult. Just as Greek art, in its perfection and incapacity of being transcended, had a deathly influence upon the art of Europe, and just as the music of Bach makes all that has been composed since him superfluous and frivolous or artificial, so Chinese Zen made all later Zen, as religion, imitative and second hand. But that is not what I really wanted to say, which is this. A thing that comes into existence, by its very existence, prevents itself from coming into existence. What is good, what is really good is what is about to come into existence, the ZEN which is not yet Zen. (Zen may be said to exist, in some sense, in its being created by Huineng, Linchi and so on). Zen, as religion, is no longer possible, any more than Buddhism or Christianity, except as a kind of repetition, which may be Zen, but is not ZEN. Thus Zen is tinged with a certain hopelessness and nihilism, because we do not wish to repeat the discovery of other people; we wish to be the first that ever burst into that silent sea. Arnold says,

> How fair a lot to fill
> Is left to each man still.

This is true, but we do not want "a fair lot," the left-overs of other ages. Man wants what is impossible; he wants it only because, only if it is impossible. These are the authentic "airs and echoes that convey a melancholy into all our day." We must create ZEN, and perish in the attempt.

INDEX